Praise for *Creating Justice* :
Families and Multigenerati

Ministers, religious educators, and congregations have always longed for a publication like this one. We long to find ways to bring generations together and put their faith into action through projects and learning that speak to all ages. This book will be a resource for families, and also for church professionals and leaders. Thank you to the creators!

Linda Olson Peebles, Minister of Faith in Action,
Unitarian Universalist Church of Arlington, Virginia

Whether or not families are able to attend church every Sunday, many are craving resources to help their children connect with their faith all week long. This good resource is a godsend to parents who are concerned with raising moral children, and who want to embody the values of their faith community. *Creating Justice Together* inspires engagement, equips parents as religious educators in their homes, and answers the yearning to make a difference that is shared across generations.

Karen Bellavance-Grace, Director of Faith Formation,
Clara Barton & Massachusetts Bay Districts

As a religious educator, I am so grateful for this compendium of social action projects—not only as a source of ready-made "how to"s for social justice projects but for how it equips and empowers lay leaders with a framework to view and address whatever the social justice issues of their community may be.

Christopher Buja, Director of Lifespan Faith
Development, Unitarian Universalist Congregation of
Somerset Hills, Somerville, NJ

Creating Justice Together is a wonderful collection of thirty-six meaningful projects and learning experiences intended for diverse groups of people. Anyone who is eager to grow in their Unitarian Universalist identity could gather a group and use this collection to make a real difference in the world, beginning with the group members. Families, covenant groups, neighborhood circles, and even groups of UU friends might use these projects to truly grow in spirit, service, justice, and love.

> Deborah Cayer, Lead Minister, Eno River Unitarian Universalist Fellowship, Durham, NC

Creating Justice Together

Service Projects for Families and Multigenerational Groups

Edited and Introduced by Susan Dana Lawrence

Judith A. Frediani and Jessica York,
Developmental Editors

UNITARIAN UNIVERSALIST ASSOCIATION

BOSTON

Printed in the United States

6 5 4 3 2 1
16 15 14

Library of Congress Cataloging-in-Publication Data

Creating justice together : service projects for families and multigenerational groups / edited and introduced by Susan Dana Lawrence, Judith A. Frediani, and Jessica York, developmental editors.
    pages cm
  ISBN 978-1-55896-739-7 (pbk.:alk. paper) 1. Social justice—Religious aspects—Unitarian Universalist Association. I. Lawrence, Susan D., 1957- editor of compilation.
  BX9856.C74 2014
   261.8—dc23

                                              2014003087

Contents

Preface

This book curates thirty-six ways to hear the call of justice and love and give these values shape in the world. Three dozen projects from the Unitarian Universalist Association's flagship Tapestry of Faith core curricula for children, youth, adults, and multigenerational groups are repurposed here for use outside the formal, congregational religious education setting. If you are raising a Unitarian Universalist child or have a leadership role in a multiage, liberal faith-based group, the projects presented here will interest you.

As people of faith, we want to spread justice and love to people we know, our civic communities, and the world community, where so many wrongs cry out to be righted. Many of us have passion for a particular cause or concern—maybe more than one. And we do not want to just sit around and talk about righting wrongs: We want to *do* something. We seek a path of action that announces our moral imperatives and can truly make a difference. We want to do something that resonates with the faith we carry inside.

Many of us yearn not only to act, with purpose and in faith, but also to show young people how they can too. As parents and communities raising Unitarian Universalist children, we want to model and encourage ways to step up, even to act up, to share justice and love. We want projects we can do together, all ages, and we want these projects to be meaningful, fulfilling, and transformative—because we yearn not only to demonstrate faith but also to grow in faith. We understand that we can grow in faith at any age, not just childhood and youth. That is why, although sometimes the work is hard, we yearn for the challenges and learning we gain from building the respectful relationships we need to do good works in the world.

This book provides concrete help to satisfy such yearnings. The projects here invite you to live your faith in the world, share your experience with family or friends, and together articulate the questions, values, and hopes woven into your service—the reasons you do the work. Each project offers a conscious, intentional experience of faith in action for all ages, whether you cook in a homemade solar oven, write to a soldier serving overseas, or make a welcome kit for a new neighbor. Each project guides you to connect your experience with your own values and to share or journal your reflections so that your growth in faith can be rich, personal, and long lasting.

May this book call forth service and justice efforts from the depth of your convictions and caring. May you forge real connections with faith, your family, and the people near and far with whom you will partner to offer yourself in service.

In faith and with hope,
Susan Lawrence
Managing Editor, Faith Development Office
Unitarian Universalist Association

How to Use This Book

Do you belong to a Unitarian Universalist congregation? Do you consider yourself a Unitarian Universalist although you are not a member of a congregation? Maybe you have heard a bit about Unitarian Universalism and sense that you share this faith movement's perspectives and goals. Maybe you are a seeker in faith who finds resonance with Unitarian Universalist beliefs, questions, and practices —or maybe you are about to find that resonance in these pages.

Are you a parent? You may be literally raising children, or perhaps you work with young people as part of your job or belong to an extended family or community network in which you have a mentoring role. If you embrace a responsibility and seek opportunities to help guide the development of a young person's faith, spirit, and character, you will find this book both relevant and useful.

Each project offered here invites a wide age range of people to work together to promote justice and love in the world. Every effort to make the world a better place matters, and many will admire you for accomplishing that much. However, each project offers something more, a latent transformative power that you, as its leader, can activate. The projects support and guide you to not only lead a worthwhile, informative activity but also to create a deeply meaningful experience that will equip each participant, no matter how old or young, to better understand and make manifest their most heartfelt beliefs and values.

Social, economic, and environmental justice issues motivate many Unitarian Universalists to act in faith. The world's need for care, compassion, generosity, and forgiveness also motivates many. Unitarian Universalists have no religious creed, yet we are capable of questioning injustice with a fierceness to match the zeal of any religious fundamentalist. What do we fundamentally believe? We believe in humanity's capacity to change, grow, and love one another. We believe that we, as a species, can do better. These beliefs motivate us to do good. The projects in this book offer thirty-six ways for people of all ages, as a family, in an informal UU group, or on their own, to channel that motivation and intentionally live their faith.

Faith has a peculiar quality: It is a renewable resource. When we intentionally act in faith, we do not use it up. Rather, we gain an opportunity to grow it. Faith development does not come automatically, but we invite it when we enter into an act of faith aware of our purpose, engage in the work in a manner consistent with our values and Principles, and follow our action with thoughtful reflection. Unitarian Universalist religious education programs for all ages support leaders as they guide participants through this process. You will see that same model in every activity here.

The activities in this book range from personal encounters with the spirit, as in Thankful Book (page 2), to efforts to stand publicly with people struggling against injustice and striving to better their circumstances, as in Box House for Homelessness Awareness (page 40). They range from firsthand, close-range engagement with our interconnected web of life, as in Creating a Backyard Habitat (page 3), to reaching out as partners to people we are unlikely ever to meet in person, as in Microlending Abroad (page 89).

With all their diversity, the projects share a basic structure to ensure that participants deepen their faith through action. First, we articulate questions and deeply held values activated by the project. Next, we demonstrate our beliefs and pursue our questions through action. After we have acted, we evaluate the impact of our action. What difference have we made to others and to the wider worlds of community, society, and humanity? Finally, we take a moment to touch again our deeply held values and revisit our understandings of how the world works. When we articulate the impact a project has on us, we give closure to this cycle of our faith development and, at the same time, affirm that our growth in faith never has to end. This book invites and supports you to carry this dynamic faith development process beyond the context of formal Unitarian Universalist religious education programming and into your home.

The projects here were chosen and adapted from "Faith in Action" activities in the Tapestry of Faith curricula. Religious education groups using the Tapestry of Faith curricula are encouraged to make time outside their regular meetings for justice and service projects. Every Tapestry of Faith session suggests a Faith in Action project designed to extend and deepen participants' exposure to the session's themes. You can read the original descriptions of the projects suggested here online in Tapestry of Faith (**www.uua.org/tapestry**) and discover many more to adapt on your own. In the context of a curriculum, a Faith in Action project amplifies participants' learning and growth. In the context of home and family, these projects can do the same for you.

Every project in this book is suitable for a family or an informal group of UUs or like-minded fellow travelers. Many can be done by an individual. If you are involved with a UU congregation, cluster, or other community, you may find appealing projects for multigenerational midweek programming, a Sunday all-ages program, a summer camp or weekend conference, or a multiage scout troop working toward Religion in Life badges. If you are a congregational leader, consider enriching lay leadership training or a board retreat by including one of these projects.

Each project is tagged in several ways to help you choose and plan:

- **Short-term** projects can be done in one meeting or several that culminate in a central experience. **Long-term** projects happen over a longer time span and have longer-range objectives; thus, they require a greater commitment to partners and goals.
- **All ages** projects offer active roles and faith development opportunities for preschoolers through elders. A few projects likely to be doable or meaningful only for those past

early childhood or elementary age are tagged "ages six and up" or "ages ten and up." All the projects can work with a multigenerational, multiability group (which is, after all, what a family is). We encourage you to form a multiage group if you do not already share a household or family with one. Younger people benefit from working alongside older role models. People of all ages are empowered and develop a sense of personal agency by contributing their unique gifts in an age-diverse group.

- **Projects that can be done at zero-to-minimal cost** are marked "¢." If expenses could reach five dollars per person, a project is marked "$." There are a few "$$" projects for which expenses may approach twenty dollars per person, but they can be adapted for a shoestring budget.

The projects are organized in three chapters. Projects in Chapter 1, Together at Home, are designed especially for a family group. Chapter 2, Make a Difference Locally, invites your multigenerational group to act in faith to benefit your neighborhood, municipality, or another community to which you belong. Chapter 3, Citizens of the World, suggests responses to some of the world's pressing needs and affirms the importance and the potential impact of each of us doing even a little bit to help.

Each project suggests one or two faith objectives, that is, gifts of faith the project is likely to awaken in you and give you opportunities to share. The icons will help you quickly identify projects that speak to your interests:

Ecology ▨

Justice ⚖

Love ♥

Peace 🕊

Embedded in each project is spiritual as well as logistical guidance to enhance a project's meaning for you as well as its smooth implementation and positive impact in the world. First, the pragmatic: We describe the supplies, preparation, and time commitment needed and other practical considerations. Second, the spiritual: Each project leads you into a conscious faith development experience to share with children, youth, family members, or friends engaged in the project with you. You will find reflection and discussion prompts to make planning, facilitating, and processing each project a true journey in faith.

To help you articulate the religious purpose, objectives, and meaning of each project, we guide you to explore how it expresses particular UU Principles. Unitarian Universalist congregations are bound not by a single shared creed but by a covenant to affirm and promote these seven Principles:

1. The inherent worth and dignity of every person
2. Justice, equity, and compassion in human relations
3. Acceptance of one another and encouragement to spiritual growth
4. A free and responsible search for truth and meaning
5. The right of conscience and the use of the democratic process
6. The goal of world community with peace, liberty, and justice for all
7. Respect for the interdependent web of life

Each project in this book is tagged with one or more UU Principle numbers (1–7). The narrative descriptions link one or more Principles with aspects of the project. If the UU Principles are new to you, you may want to explore them further. The UUA website (www.uua.org) is a good place to start. As you become more intimate with these Principles, we hope you will begin to apply your own UU Principles checklist to the large and small ways you act in faith on a daily basis. To articulate the beliefs and hopes that motivate you to take a particular action is to engage in your own faith development. Let your faith development become a regular practice.

Covenant and Service

All service is about relationships. Between someone who wants to help and someone who needs help. Between partners in service to others or to a common cause. Between humans and other life with which we share Earth's interconnected web. Between oneself and one's faith, truth, or God.

In Unitarian Universalism, relationships are grounded in covenant, and our covenants, in turn, are grounded in our values. We make a covenant to bring core values such as respect, compassion, and open-mindedness into all aspects of a relationship. For example, members of a Unitarian Universalist committee or religious education group might typically covenant to arrive prepared and on time, to "step back or step up" so quieter voices can find space in a discussion, or to avoid making assumptions about other members based on perceptions and biases.

You may not have an opportunity to create a covenant with your partners in a justice or service project. However, you can and should be mindful of the promises implicit in a Unitarian Universalist service project—again, respect, compassion, and open-mindedness. This chapter guides you to incorporate UU values into the project you will do with your family or group using four key strategies: Include all ages; plan for accessibility and inclusion; look through an antiracist, multicultural, antioppression lens; and partner in right relationship.

Include All Ages

A decision to act for justice and love as a multiage group has the potential to bring Unitarian Universalist values to life in a way that will enrich each and all of you. How you work together can be as powerful a faith development experience as the service project itself. Ensure a positive experience for all ages by intentionally applying UU Principles in your choice of a project and individual roles, safety considerations, and opportunities for all ages to meaningfully process the project.

Choosing a Project

Follow your heart, your head, and your realistic assessment of your family or group members' availability and willingness to participate. If gathering everyone together multiple times will be difficult, select a project conducive to individuals or subgroups doing some preparation and implementation steps separately. The most important times to be together are the meeting in which you introduce and begin the project and the meeting to share your experiences and reflections afterward.

Choose projects that invite children to grow in faith and understanding while they have fun actively *doing*. Some children will enjoy a role decorating a poster, arranging merchandise or flyers on a display table, writing a letter, or counting and recounting money your project may earn. Others may like to be creative or productive in a team that is building, cleaning, or problem solving. Try to provide a variety of tasks to appeal to participants with many different interests. Some children who appear to be quietly coming along, or "not participating," may indeed be fully engaged in their kind of action. You may see the evidence later when you share a reflection process together.

Because we value the inherent worth and dignity of each person, we take care to honor the abilities and gifts of the youngest among us, our elders, and everyone in between. When you introduce a project, explain as clearly as you can the tasks involved. Youth, adults, and elders will usually recognize and claim a role for themselves, whereas children tend to "vote with their feet" once an activity is underway. As much as possible, allow people to choose how they will participate. This does not mean that no one should do anything challenging or tedious. Encourage participants who step outside their comfort zone to complete tasks that might seem daunting, and be prepared to provide support. If too many members of your group resist particular jobs, invite everyone to help solve the problem of how, together, you will make sure those unappealing tasks get done.

Engage every member of your group in all three phases of a project: preparation, doing, and reflection. Many projects in this book use the headings "Before," "The Project," and "After" to outline these phases. From the start, involve everyone in some aspect of planning. While logistics must usually be arranged by an adult or a capable youth, a young child can and should contribute to selecting a project, researching the problem your project addresses, and making concrete choices as your plan takes shape. A child can decide whether the group will use large or small boxes to pack books for incarcerated prisoners (Dignity Behind Bars, page 59) or what kind of snack to bring for children living at a family shelter (A Voice for Children, page 34). Giving children important choices to make empowers them as agents and can be a strong force pulling them into the project.

The activities offer an array of roles suitable for various ages and levels of maturity. As a leader, you will have different tasks than a young child, including some tasks only an adult or older youth can do. However, it is essential that you spend some time working in proximity to the child, if not together at the same task. When you work alongside a child, you teach by modeling the compassionate, justice-seeking attitudes and actions you hope they will emulate.

Short-term projects can be rewarding, especially with children, because they offer instant gratification such as shared smiles and thanks. Long-term projects lengthen and perhaps deepen your encounter with the real problems of other people, your community, or our world. Consequently, experiences, reactions, and reflections will be more complex and potentially richer; you will need to provide more time for processing.

Starting projects without assumptions applies to the older members of your group too. Older members may relish the opportunity to engage in ways they typically do not. They might enjoy coloring alongside young members or using desktop-publishing skills to design flyers.

Safety and Legal Considerations

Common sense will keep all ages safe when a project takes place in your home. When a project brings your family or group into a public space or on-site at a service agency, you will need to be vigilant to ensure that children are supervised. Make sure your group's ratio of older, mature group members to young children is adequate for the environment. When your family or group will join a larger group in a physically expansive area—for example, to participate in a Peace Pinwheel Vigil or Parade (page 81) or an Audubon Bird Count (page 69)—use a buddy system so that every young person has at least one older person aware of where they are at all times.

If you plan to visit a direct service organization, such as a homeless shelter, soup kitchen, or retirement home, find out in advance what restrictions apply. Confirm that the facility welcomes children of the ages in your group, and ask where children will be allowed to go on-site and what they may have an opportunity to do. Make sure the site will be accessible to everyone with the range of mobility in your group. You may need to secure a parent's written permission if you plan to bring along a minor child or youth who is not yours. Ask a site manager if there are any items you are not permitted to bring into a facility. Clarify the policy on taking photos or video—client service agencies may ask you not to. Generally a service provider agency will not allow you to photograph clients, and they absolutely will not without signed consent.

In a multigenerational group activity, make courtesy the rule and be explicit about how to show it to ensure everyone's physical comfort and safety. For example, if you are working in a tight space, do not allow children to run around where they might knock into someone moving at a slower pace or using a walker or cane. Tell people where to put coats, personal items, and project supplies so they do not block others' passage through the room. You might wish to use a talking stick—or another object that gives the holder the right to speak—to encourage taking turns in a discussion, or ask everyone to avoid side conversations so people with hearing difficulties can fully participate. Anticipate that younger children may have trouble occupying themselves quietly during a discussion or a sedentary activity, and ask parents or older youth to help by engaging children with soft, quiet "fidget objects," such as pipe cleaners or clay, or taking restless children temporarily to another space.

Creating a Meaningful Process

The three-step process of preparation, implementation, and reflection serves project participants of any age, yet you can and should design each step to suit your group. For all ages, and particularly for children, a well-chosen story is an effective way to introduce a problem, awaken an emotional response, and prompt a group to think of actions to advance a solution. Several projects in this book include stories from Tapestry of Faith curricula and provide guidance for using the story with the project. On the UUA's Tapestry of Faith main web page (**www.uua.org/tapestry**), you can use the search function to identify additional, potentially relevant stories by keyword or theme.

You can also generate interest in a project by sharing a story from real life. Many of the organizations whose websites we provide publish case studies that illustrate how they support people as they face challenges. Some organizations provide information and stories specifically for children. If online research will focus your family or group on a service or justice opportunity, browse for stories together. However, visit the websites ahead of time to make sure the material is useful as well as suitable for children.

When you use a story to introduce a project, take time to unpack the story carefully so that children understand what is real, what is metaphor, and what is fantasy. Help children name the important themes in the story, like protecting the earth, standing up for justice, or helping one another. Explain how the story connects with the real issue you want your family or group to tackle. Then get to the concrete project at hand: What is the situation? What needs to change? What can be done to bring change, and how can your family help?

You can be candid with children but do not overwhelm them with dire statistics or gratuitously shocking details of an unfair or violent situation. The projects in this book offer language to help you describe some of the world's problems and suggest some reasons and ways our faith calls us to address these problems. Your explanations need not be elaborate. Avoid oversimplifying, but keep it simple. Do not underestimate children's capacity to recognize an injustice and understand why it is wrong. As you investigate homelessness, persistent racism, discrimination against immigrants, legalized cruelty to animals, climate change, or inequities in the global distribution of schooling, clean water, and other resources, children's questions may cut to the heart of an injustice in a way that deepens the faith development experience for all of you.

When you process a service or justice experience afterward, use your instincts to determine what your family or group needs to talk about beyond what the provided reflection questions offer. The questions are designed to prompt all ages to connect their experiences with their feelings, values, and faith. However, do not be disappointed if your reflection time does not immediately produce an amazing discussion (though sometimes it will). Put some questions out there. Give your family or group time to sit with their thoughts.

Plan for Accessibility and Inclusion

Plan projects thoughtfully to ensure they will be accessible physically and have the potential to be spiritually meaningful for every member of your group. To do this, you will need to pay attention to the unique set of abilities and gifts each person in your family or group brings. Acknowledge too that members may have different reasons for doing a project, different time constraints for participating, or even different ways of relating to its religious significance. Consider how you can accommodate everyone.

In a Unitarian Universalist group, diversities in ability, theology, and age add a dimension to the faith development a service project offers. To recognize and embrace differences within our group is to enact the radical welcome and respectful inclusion suggested by our first Principle, that each person is important and deserves respect, and our second Principle, which points us toward justice, equity, and compassion. Our ability to accept one another and support one another's spiritual growth is affirmed by our third Principle. The more intentionally you build a strong foundation of inclusion in your group, the more authentically you will embody your own religious values and the more powerfully your faith will grow as you do the project together.

All of the projects in this book can be adapted to accommodate individuals' physical limitations or disabilities. If a project involves any sort of traveling—and most do—make sure the places you want to go are accessible to everyone who will come with you. When reading or writing are involved, partner a pre-reader or less confident reader with a strong reader, someone who likes writing things down with someone who does not. Never set up a situation in which people are expected to read unfamiliar text aloud; always ask for volunteer readers and, whenever possible, give volunteers an advance peek at the text they will read. With art activities, set expectations broadly and take care to acknowledge everyone's contribution. One project, Night Sky Adventure (page 91), asks everyone to actively observe and to question what they see. The project includes an alternate approach so that someone with a vision disability can be guided to observe and wonder using other senses.

When you form your own group for a service project, particularly if you are a family, you probably know the culture and identity of every member. Even so, some identities may be invisible to you, so do not assume you know how everyone thinks or feels. When you discuss a service opportunity, take care to avoid *us* and *them* language. If you emphasize the otherness of people you wish to partner with and help, you work against the very values that led you into the project and risk alienating someone in your group who identifies with an aspect of the problem you wish to help solve.

For example, the Living Simply project (page 72) asks everyone to voluntarily give up entertainment, food, or other services they do not really need and donate equivalent funds to people who are less materially advantaged. Do not make suggestions as to what expenses are "extra" and what comforts are "easy" to give up based solely on your own norms of spending or level of material comfort. As with race/ethnicity, level of education, gender identity, sexual orientation, theology, and many other aspects of our identities, it is always best to assume diversity in a group with regard to financial status. Your group may include more economic disparity than you know. Avoid language that assumes all members share a common financial situation, such as, "Of course, none of us have ever been homeless," or "In our town, we all have lots of food to eat."

Look Through an Antiracist, Multicultural, Anti-oppression Lens

The idea of beloved community, lifted up by Rev. Dr. Martin Luther King, Jr., resonates strongly with our Unitarian Universalist Principles, especially the sixth, the goal of world community with peace, liberty, and justice for all. When we put our faith into action in accord with the values that undergird our Principles, we move the world forward toward beloved community. To truly live our UU values, we must do so with an antiracist, multicultural, anti-oppression lens.

When you take on a project that involves only your family, you may be aware of diverse identities. However, when you include others—say, from your congregation or community—in a project, anticipate cultural differences and identities that may not be obvious. You will need to be more intentional yet in your inclusiveness.

Start by expecting diversity: Everyone in your group will have different life experiences and may bring different cultural expectations with them. Watch for assumptions on your part. For example, if your group is taking part in Welcome Kits (page 38), do not make assumptions about what local restaurants your new neighbors might enjoy based on their ethnicity or include a card with an illustration of people of a specific race or ethnicity. If giving toys is part of your plan for A Voice for Children (page 34), buy stuffed animals instead of dolls to avoid racial connotations. If you will play board games, stay away from those that do not include ethnic diversity. When seeking interviewees for Families Far and Near (page 85), do not assume that a person of color is more likely to be a recent immigrant than a white person.

Living our first Principle means modeling respect in all our actions. If you decide to sing an African-American spiritual at a peace rally, do so respectfully; share the history of the song and acknowledge that its meaning may not be the same for everyone. If your planning group includes African Americans, ask them how they feel about using the song and respect their wishes. Help even the youngest member of your family or group understand cultural misappropriation. Search **www.uua.org** for more information.

As you engage with injustice in the world, be prepared for children to ask questions about what they see. They might ask, "Why do only Asian Americans live in this neighborhood?" or "Why are we always donating money for food to Africa?" Be prepared to answer these questions as honestly as you can on a level that is appropriate for the age of the child. You can admit that sometimes there is no one answer. For example, you might suggest, "It is possible that the Asian-American people who live here enjoy living near others who share their culture. It also may be that the real estate community shows Asian Americans places to live in this neighborhood and does not show these homes to other ethnicities." You can teach your child that hunger is not confined to other continents by collecting money to help a rural U.S. community in need.

Your actions may take you to communities of people who are different from you. Children notice differences. Remember that there is nothing wrong with noticing differences; bias, prejudice, and discrimination arise when value judgments are attached to differences. When a child remarks on a difference, saying that "That person is just like us" is disingenuous. To avoid acknowledging differences might make them seem shameful or bad to a young child. Confirm differences. Then ask, "Do you think their skin color means they are not a good person?" or say "They use a wheelchair, but I think they have just as much right to shop anywhere they want. Do you?" We can teach children to respect and value differences and also to understand that everyone has a right to meet their basic human needs.

The activities in this book do not necessarily call you to work with people who are different from you. Nonetheless, you can make that choice. Should you choose to partner with other groups, you might intentionally partner with people who are different from you and your family or group in age, race or ethnicity, ability, gender identity, affectional or sexual orientation, social or economic class, or first language. If you do, the work to build beloved community across these differences could enrich the experience and call for a deeper engagement with our faith and its values of respect, love, empathy, and inclusivity.

Partnering in Right Relationship

Our first UU Principle proclaims the inherent worth and dignity of every person. Our fourth UU Principle affirms that everyone should have a voice in matters that concern them. Let these values guide your first steps into a service project. Do not assume you know what someone else needs. Instead, ask. Start with a question, such as "How can we help?" When working with a new community, ask the community to identify the spokespeople or leaders you should work with, understanding that this does not mean that the community is homogeneous or always of the same opinion.

When the UU congregation of Honolulu, Hawaii, reached out to help a rural community in the Philippines, they quickly learned that the first step would have to be a conversation about what the community needed. Leaders from the First Unitarian Church of Honolulu and leaders from the Unitarian Universalist Church of Caican interviewed residents of Caican and held community meetings. Once the community identified clean water as its most pressing need, the partnership really took off. Caican residents elected a committee of leaders to oversee the project. Together, the committee and leaders of the two UU congregations researched solutions to the water problem. Once a solution was found, Hawaiian UUs helped raise money to dig a well, while local residents managed the process on-site. The money alone would not have solved the problem. The Caican community's buy-in of the project resulted in an investment of time and expertise, which made the project successful.

When you engage in direct service work, acting in right relationship requires special preparation. For adults as well as youth and children, it can be confusing or discomfiting to enter into a situation in which hope and hardship meet. To witness need, pain, or despair close-up can sometimes trigger disgust or judgmental feelings. In response, some of us may instinctively pull back into an observer role, while others may push forward to make a personal connection with service recipients. If you plan to serve a meal at a soup kitchen, tutor homeless children living in a family shelter, or bring donated supplies to the site of a recent disaster or an animal shelter, use the planning phase for spiritual as well as practical preparation. Emphasize the universality across human experience of sometimes being one who needs and sometimes being one who helps: This time, you are bringing your hands, hearts, and minds into a situation where your gifts can help others; another time, someone else's hands, heart, and mind will help you. Learn as much as you can about what you will see, hear, and experience on-site. Some organizations offer training or orientation that unpacks the context in which they work and teaches participants what to expect. Plan in advance how you will process the site visit afterward and make sure everyone knows they will have this processing opportunity.

Even when your service work does not bring you into direct contact with a recipient, you can still partner with them. Some organizations such as the Unitarian Universalist Service Committee, Habitat for Humanity, and Kiva (a microfinance organization) will have already respectfully inquired about what is needed and how outsiders can help. You can step into a preexisting right relationship when you engage in one of their projects. The websites, reports, and fundraising materials provided by these organizations emphasize the agency of the people who receive help. Browsing these sites will help you learn about the problems and opportunities to which the organization responds and invite you into the mind-set of right relationship. Read stories of people who have changed their own lives with the organization's help and solutions that they devised for themselves and retain ownership of. When your gift is monetary, you are not giving charity; rather, you are facilitating justice by taking action to redistribute the world's wealth more equitably.

You may find yourself working alongside people of another faith or people whose purpose or approach to the service project seems to differ from yours. Accept the differences. Emphasize the common impulse for good that brings you together.

Ecology projects express the deep covenant many Unitarian Universalists feel with our living planet. Our seventh Principle says that we humans are just one component of the complex system that is life on earth. We know we have much power to restore balances that previous generations have upset, and we accept that responsibility as Unitarian Universalists. Some UUs would say that when we step up as stewards of ecological balance, we act as partners of God, the universe, the Spirit of Life, or the Great Mystery. Most would agree that environmental justice work invites us into right relationship with the interconnected web.

The ultimate partnership in service work is the one you form with the faith inside yourself. What motivates you to act? What outcomes do you believe are possible? A decision to put your faith into action offers a unique opportunity to articulate it, know it, and grow it. Use the guidance we provide for *Before*, *The Project*, and *After* to keep connected to the meaning, purpose, and faith development possibilities of your project throughout the three phrases of planning, action, and reflection.

A service project can energize or sharply test your faith in justice or human capability. Some projects will do both. However, a feeling of completion, appreciation, learning, spiritual zest—or even spiritual doubt—does not by itself constitute faith development. Your effort to do good does *you* the most good when you intentionally reflect on it and use your reflections to inform your future actions. The projects guide your group to process your experiences, together with prompts to help you articulate your actions as expressions of your values and beliefs, make meaning of the work you have done, and plan ways to extend the work.

If you undertake a project on your own, journal about it. Talk about it with friends. If a group project, plan to share refreshments or a meal together immediately following your last meeting. Choose a location conducive to focused, private conversation. With family members, you might have the conversation on a bus coming home or at bedtime some days later. Include questions to refresh everyone's memories of the experience. Move on to questions such as, "How will this experience change my future beliefs and actions?" Be sure to have the conversation.

TOGETHER AT HOME

Together at Home

1. Thankful Book

UU Principles 1, 2, 3

Long-term / All ages / $

Start a nighttime ritual of naming the things you are thankful for before going to bed. Each person can speak their list aloud to a family member, think it just to themselves, or write it in a Thankful Book kept near their bed. Older family members can help younger family members write. Try to list at least five things each day and include one thing that is different each day. You can always write "family," but encourage everyone to be more specific. Maybe one particular day you are thankful for the particular way a person helped you—a family member, a classmate, a colleague, or a worker at a store or library.

Variation: Did you help someone today? Perhaps you are thankful for being given the opportunity to help someone. Try, at least one night a week, to recall a service you are thankful you were able to provide and add it to your Thankful Book or nighttime ritual. Does this addition make you more mindful of your daily actions toward others?

From *Love Surrounds Us* Session 10 (Our Words Matter), Tapestry of Faith for grades K/1

2. Creating a Backyard Habitat

UU Principles 3, 5, 7

Long-term / All ages / $$

You will need:

- Seedlings for local plants that provide food or shelter for animals (like butterfly bush, milkweed, or berry shrubs)
- Outdoor containers for fresh water (e.g., fountain, bird-bath,)
- Digging tools and watering cans
- Optional: items to shelter animals, such as a birdhouse or a bat box

Before. Identify a part of your backyard or a porch or windowsill to convert to a wildlife habitat. Investigate local wildlife needs by consulting government or conservation agencies, such as the Environmental Protection Agency or the Audubon Society or your local park board. Identify beneficial plants and trees that would support local wildlife. One good resource is the National Wildlife Federation website, where you can also certify your habitat: **www.nwf.org/gardenforwildlife**.

Plan a date to begin building the habitat and pencil in subsequent dates to regather and continue the job. Take the time to devise meaningful, appropriate tasks for people of all ages and abilities. Invite more people to help and turn the project into a party. Obtain the materials you will need.

The Project. Create a backyard habitat by installing a fountain or birdbath, making and placing a birdhouse or other animal shelter, or planting seedlings. Make this a fifth Principle project by giving everyone a voice in making decisions and choosing tasks, while taking care that the scope of the project is not too ambitious and that each person has a role they can enjoy and satisfactorily accomplish.

While working, snacking, or resting, create conversation about how making a backyard habitat reflects Unitarian Universalist beliefs:

- How does this project help us fulfill our seventh Principle, respect for the interdependent web of life?
- How are we living our third and fifth Principles by doing this project?
- What do we hope will happen in our backyard habitat?

After. Make a schedule that specifies ways each individual will help maintain or observe the habitat. Maintenance tasks might include filling bird feeders, cleaning/filling a birdbath, protecting plants from cold before winter, or planting seeds in spring. Observation tasks might include counting or identifying birds, alerting the group to changes or damage in the habitat, or photographing animals that visit.

You can order a "certified wildlife habitat" sign from the National Wildlife Federation (**www.nwf.org**). Hold a family ritual to dedicate your habitat when the sign arrives. Include a reading from one of our UU Sources of wisdom: Hinduism (third Source, world religions) offers the concept of *ahimsa* (doing no harm) and respect for animals; reason and science (fifth Source) help us understand what wild animals need to survive and why our habitat needs the animals; earth-centered religions (sixth Source) speak about balance and harmony in nature.

Nurturing a backyard habitat takes much less time than building one. What more can you do to support local wildlife? To encourage others in your community to create their own backyard habitats?

From *Love Will Guide Us* Session 10 (Love For All Creatures), Tapestry of Faith for grades 2/3

3. Recycled Art

UU Principles 4, 7

Short-term / All ages / $

You will need:

- Clean, recyclable items such as paper towel tubes, magazines, fabric scraps, sea shells, broken parts from games or toys, used food containers
- Art supplies such as paper, scissors, glue, tape, markers, and craft sticks

Before. Find examples of creative reuse of materials that otherwise might go into landfills as trash; birds' nests provide a great example in nature. Read Janeen Grohsmeyer's "The Most Beautiful Bower in the World," reprinted below from the Tapestry of Faith program *World of Wonder*. Consider inspiring children by sharing this story. You may find inspiration on the website of the annual Recycled Arts Festival in Vancouver, Washington (**www.recycledartsfestival.com**). If how-to ideas will spark imagination, look at "Recycled Crafts: Turning Trash into Children's Treasures" (**www.pbs.org/parents**) or collect examples to share with the group, such as collages, sculptures, and functional objects such as pencil holders. Collect and clean recyclable materials.

Locally, you may be able to purchase industrial throwaways to use for craft making. The nonprofit Extras for Creative Reuse (www.extrasforcreativereuse.org/) supplies the Boston public schools and sells materials to members.

The Project. Follow our fourth Unitarian Universalist Principle, our search for truth and meaning, into a wider understanding of *recycling*. To introduce creative reuse, offer an example, such as how birds gather items that had a different original purpose and give them new life as part of a nest. Invite everyone to use the materials you have provided, in any way they wish, to create a work of art. The artwork might also be an item of use. Show or describe any examples you collected. Invite everyone to be as imaginative as possible; there is no right or wrong way to be artistic. Recycled art made with a special recipient in mind can be a way to share love, creativity, and an affirmation of the responsibility for environmental stewardship we all share.

After. Point out how each artist's creative energy has added value to items that might otherwise be thrown away. Does an item need to have a function to be useful? Speculate about what each piece of artwork wants to say: What is its message and what truth does it share? Display art in your home or give it as a gift. See if everyone can think of a different way that repurposing potential trash into art honors the interdependent web. Reducing landfill is one way— but there are more.

From *World of Wonder* Session 9 (Creativity in Nature), Tapestry of Faith for grades K/1

Story: The Most Beautiful Bower in the World

By Janeen Grohsmeyer

In the land of Australia, where koalas climb high in eucalyptus trees and kangaroos bound across grassy plains on great big feet, a baby bird pecked his way out of his shell.

His mother called him Kejaro and she brought him good fruit to eat. Every day, for dessert, she brought him bugs. His feathers were brown and green, just like his mother's. Both Kejaro and his mother had pale blue eyes.

Every day, Kejaro ate fruit and bugs, to help him grow bigger. Every day, he flapped his wings hard, to help him grow stronger.

And every night, his mother told him stories about his father. "He was handsome, with satiny blue feathers," she told him. "He was graceful, with a beautiful dance. He was charming, with a lovely voice. And he built the most beautiful bower in the world."

"What's a bower?" asked Kejaro, for all he knew of the world was their nest, high in a tree and surrounded by green leaves, and the slivers of blue far above them that his mother said was "sky."

"A bower is a special nest, built on the ground," his mother told him. "With his feet, your father smoothed the ground to make a dancing floor. With his beak, he placed each twig, just so, to make an archway. He chewed leaves and berries to make paint, then dipped a piece of bark into it and painted the archway's walls. He flew far and wide to find the prettiest flowers and feathers and shells to decorate the bower with, and all of them were of the most beautiful blue."

"Like the sky?" Kejaro asked.

"Like the sky," his mother agreed. "When I came to the bower, your father danced and sang for me, and then I joined him on the dancing floor. Someday, Kejaro, you will build a bower for your lady love."

Then his mother covered him with her wing, for it was time to sleep. Kejaro closed his eyes, wondering what kind of bower he would build when he was grown.

When Kejaro was three weeks old, he flew for the very first time. Soon, he could swoop and soar and zoom up and zoom down. He went high enough to see the sky, and it was huge. It stretched from one end of the world to the other, and all of it was of the most beautiful blue.

A few days later, he and his mother left their nest. They flew until they found a flock of other birds. All of them had brown and green feathers and pale blue eyes.

Kejaro spent his days playing with his new friends. They flew high in the sky, zipping and zooming and swooping and soaring. They ate fruit from trees and bushes. Sometimes, for dessert, they would hunt bugs. At night, they slept on the branches of trees. Around them, koalas climbed high in the eucalyptus trees and kangaroos bounded across the grassy plains on great big feet.

When Kejaro was five years old, he noticed that he had some new feathers that were a dark, satiny blue. The other boys had some new dark feathers, too. All the girls' were still green and brown. Kejaro decided he didn't want to spend his days zipping and zooming and swooping and soaring.

He wanted to build.

Kejaro flew into the forest, searching for just the right spot. He found it, surrounded by four tall trees, with a little rivulet of water not far away. With his feet, he smoothed the ground to make a dancing floor. With his beak, he placed each twig, just so, to make an archway. He chewed leaves and berries to make paint, then used a piece of bark to paint the archway's walls. He flew far and wide to find the prettiest flowers and feathers and shells to decorate his bower with, and all of them were of the most beautiful blue.

Every day, he noticed that more of his own feathers were turning satiny blue. Every day, he practiced dancing and singing, making the sounds of other creatures he heard. Every day, he smoothed the dancing floor and rearranged the flowers and feathers and shells.

Some days he went hunting for more decorations. Kejaro found snail shells and bright leaves and beetle wings, but he liked blue parrot feathers the best. He took a few from another bird's bower a few flights away. The next day when he came back from a trip, every single one of his blue parrot feathers were gone. So Kejaro went searching again.

In the spring, a lovely green and brown bird with pale blue eyes came to his bower. He danced and sang his best for her, but then she flew away.

Kejaro was sad, but he promised himself, "I'll do it better next time." All that next year he built and rebuilt his bower, painting the archway, smoothing the dancing floor, finding and arranging his decorations of the most beautiful blue. Almost half of his own feathers were satiny blue now, and he practiced his singing and his dancing, too.

That spring, three birds came to his bower, and he sang and danced for each of them. Two of them left when he was finished, and one of them stayed for a little while, but none of them joined him on the dancing floor.

Once again, Kejaro was sad, but once again he promised himself: "I'll do it better next time." All that year he worked hard, trying to build the most beautiful bower in the world. When spring came again, all of his own feathers were dark satiny blue. He gleamed in the sunshine, and his eyes were as blue as the sky.

One morning, a lovely green and brown bird with pale blue eyes came to his bower. She watched as he danced and sang his best for her. Kejaro finished his song and waited, hoping she thought he was handsome and graceful and charming, hoping she would stay.

She hopped over to him and said, "My name is Camira."

"My name is Kejaro," he told her, wondering if she would be his lady love.

Camira fluttered her wings a little and said, "You have built the most beautiful bower in the world."

And Kejaro was happy, for that meant he had finally done it right this time.

Then he was happier still, for Camira joined him on the dancing floor, and the two of them danced together inside the most beautiful bower in the world.

4. Seven Cents a Day

UU Principles 1, 2, 6

Long-term / Ages 6 and up / ¢

You will need:

- A calculator, paper, and pencils
- A clear jar with a lid in which you can cut a hole
- A marker to write on the jar
- 7 pennies for each person
- Paper penny rolls

Before. Identify a food bank or an agency that distributes free food in your community. Find out how their programs use donated funds and confirm that you can donate money in person; find out if they require a check or will accept cash. Get a clean, lidded jar for collecting pennies, and cut a coin-deposit slot in the lid.

The Project. This home-based fundraising project helps all ages in your family or household understand the overwhelming problem of world hunger while experiencing a personal, small-scale way to make a difference. Engaging in hunger relief together helps each person internalize our second Principle of justice, peace, and compassion in our communities and our sixth Principle, which extends this hope and care into the world. Ask everyone to imagine feeling hungry. Explain that to feel hungry for an hour or even a day is different from going weeks or months without enough of the right kinds of food to be healthy. Share examples of specific families or communities that have a serious hunger problem and brainstorm reasons this can happen: lack of money to buy food, a drought or tornado so crops cannot grow, no way to grow one's own food, lack of jobs and therefore lack of money, lack of healthy foods available where they live.

Now get out the calculator(s), paper, and pencils. Say that a few years ago, world leaders wondered how much money would be needed to cut in half the number of people living in poverty and hunger. They calculated that the goal could be achieved if every person in the United States gave seven cents a day to help. Do some number crunching to figure out what seven cents a day adds up to. How much could one person save in one week? the month of February? one year? between today and the youngest person in the room's thirtieth birthday? Help young children understand that taking on this project will not end world hunger, but your contributions will help feed some people.

What might your family give up to put aside seven cents a day per person? Make individual and group commitments to cut specific expenses in order to save the money. Label the jar, decide where to keep it, and create a schedule, and perhaps a ritual, for regularly adding pennies. For example, take a few minutes together at dinnertime, when everyone can say what they gave up that day to set aside seven cents.

After. After thirty days, open the jar and count and roll the pennies. Visit a bank to exchange the rolled coins for bills or a check. Then bring your donation to the food bank or meal-serving agency. Afterward, decide whether to continue giving seven cents a day. Discuss why individuals do or do not want to. What does it mean to them? What has the world gained through their seven-cent contributions? What have they lost by giving up seven cents of their daily expenditures? What have they gained? Do they believe their donation spreads justice and compassion? Do they believe it can alleviate anyone's hunger? Do they feel more, or less, hopeful after visiting the food bank or agency? If anyone expresses discouragement about the good their donation will do, encourage conversation about alternate actions you could take to fight hunger, and make a commitment together to take additional action.

From *Windows and Mirrors* Session 2 (Me in Faith Community, Faith Community in Me), Tapestry of Faith for grades 4/5

5. Stand on Holy Ground

UU Principles 3, 7

Short-term / All ages / ¢

In the Bible, when Moses encounters God in the form of a burning bush, God tells him, "Take off your shoes, for the place on which you are standing is holy ground." Invite your family into a sacred moment outdoors. Invite everyone to take off their shoes and feel the ground under their feet. Imagine that your feet are growing roots, spreading out under the earth. Imagine that your roots entangle with the roots of the trees and plants around you, joining you in an underground web of connection. Ask everyone to share what makes this ground seem sacred or special to them. Invite everyone to name one action they take or will take to help preserve the sacred ground. It could be not littering or helping to water plants and flowers. End your ritual by thanking the earth for holding you and the plants for supporting you.

From *Sing to the Power* Session 1 (The Power of Earth), Tapestry of Faith for grades 4/5

6. "Love Your Neighbor" Greeting Cards

UU Principles 2, 3

Short-term / All ages / $

Make and deliver a greeting card to encourage someone you do not know very well. Guide children to choose a person or family facing a challenge. Who in your neighborhood or community might appreciate encouragement at this time? Is there a child who has been teased or bullied at school, or a family experiencing a household crisis or loss? Let each individual choose the person they will make a card for; if appropriate, you can all work together on one card. Make sure the card's message names specific positive qualities of the recipient. The important thing is to create and deliver a card that will affirm the recipient's inherent worth and dignity and assure them that they are part of a caring community. To show someone you believe they can get through a challenge is to live our second and third Principles: sharing compassion and giving a spiritual boost to someone in your community. Point out that spending time to make and deliver a card can say as much to the recipient as the words you write, and that to notice and respond when someone needs encouragement is precisely what our third Unitarian Universalist Principle asks us to do.

Deliver greeting cards in person, if possible. This provides another opportunity to connect to the recipient.

Afterward, discuss the activity. Ask:

- Will our encouragement make a difference and help someone face a challenge?
- Could our action have other, far-reaching effects? Perhaps the person for whom we made a card will be inspired to do the same for someone else.

From *Love Connects Us* Session 4 (Love Your Neighbor as Yourself), Tapestry of Faith for grades 4/5

7. Create a Sacred Place: Family Altar

UU Principles 1, 3, 7

Long-term / All ages / $

You will need:

- A decorative cloth
- A chalice or candle or LED candle
- Photographs and objects of your choice

Before. Identify a place in your home for an altar—a shared sacred space. It can be in a private, quiet corner or in a common room where you often gather. Spread a decorative cloth and set a chalice or candle on the cloth.

The Project. Create an altar together. A family altar shows your acceptance of one another and encouragement of one another's spiritual growth (our third UU Principle). It also affirms each person's worth (first Principle) and the web of all life to which each of us is connected (seventh Principle). Explain that an altar is a place we make sacred by our intention and that we show our intention by placing particular items on the altar. Unitarian Universalists who use altars draw from a variety of faith and cultural traditions, including our own; UU worship spaces often include a chalice.

What items can you bring into the space to make it special with your intention? One family member might use the altar to stay connected to nature and add a seashell or leaf. Others might honor connections to ancestors—family ancestors, faith ancestors from our Unitarian Universalist past, or ancestors through adoption, marriage, a shared community or cause, or another connection meaningful to someone in your family. Include a role model or teacher with a photograph or an object that reminds you of them. Place a chime if you wish to use the altar in meditation. Use soft music and light to create a worshipful atmosphere as you set up the altar together.

After. Return to the altar again and again. Some people sit quietly, meditate, write, or draw in a journal, or do yoga at an altar. You can visit the altar to calm yourself or to energize and inspire yourself. When you make time to be with yourself in a place you have designated sacred, you honor your own inherent worth and dignity with spiritual self-care. You can visit the altar with others as well. Could you meet at the altar for a regular family ritual? That is one way to express our third Principle: Encourage one another on each of your individual journeys of spiritual growth. The altar need not stay the same forever. Change the objects on it when the focus of your faith or spirituality shifts, if doing so feels right, to refresh your altar's sacred intention.

From *Spirit of Life* Workshop 7 (Roots Hold Me Close: Tradition, Teachers, and Spiritual Formation), Tapestry of Faith for adults; *Creating Home* Session 9 (Our Ancestral Home), Tapestry of Faith for grades K/1; and *UU World* Families pages, Summer 2013

8. Solar Oven Workshop

UU Principles 4, 7

Short-term / All ages / $

You will need:

- A cardboard pizza box, newspapers, a ruler, a marker, a box knife or sharp scissors, aluminum foil, black construction paper, clear plastic wrap, tape, and glue
- A tall straw, a wooden spoon, or a stick
- A tin pie plate or glass dish, and oven mitts
- Food to cook in a solar oven, such as graham crackers, marshmallows, and chocolate bars for s'mores; tortillas and cheese for quesadillas; or hot dogs

Before. Read the instructions for making a solar oven, below. Plan roles to suit the ages and abilities in your family or group. Set up a worktable to make a solar oven and choose a full-sun outdoor place to cook.

Familiarize yourself with the benefits of solar cooking. If you have the option to cook with electrical appliances, using a solar cooker instead is a way to avoid unsustainable energy consumption and to model caring for the earth. However, for people who do not have electricity but live in a climate with abundant sun, solar oven cooking can be a practical, everyday choice that improves the health and well-being of family members as well as the earth.

Solar Cookers International (SCI) is a nonprofit organization that works to improve household and environmental conditions by promoting "free, zero-emissions energy" solar cooking technology in areas where people traditionally have used open fires for cooking and water purification. SCI and their local partners help families from Afghanistan to Zimbabwe to begin using solar ovens—made with inexpensive materials and simple techniques similar to those you will use for your backyard solar oven—to clean their drinking water and heat their food, rather than using an open fire. Reliance on open fires can be time-consuming, expensive, and dangerous. When a family cannot afford to buy firewood, several members may spend hours each day collecting wood to burn. In many places, the task of collecting firewood falls to women and children, who are vulnerable walking out on their own, especially in rural areas affected by war where government instability may lead to high crime rates.

One example of the multiple benefits solar cookers can provide is the Solar Cooker Project in the Iridimi Refugee Camp, Chad, where 14,000 cookers are operated daily. Women and children no longer have to venture far from the camp to search for firewood, risking attack. Because they do not have to spend hours looking for firewood and tending fires, the women have more time for taking care of other family needs. The ability to cleanse the water and the reduction in smoke have improved the health of residents. This project has established a solar cooker production workshop for women, and an added benefit is that women earn money from the workshop, making cookers for new residents and facilitating workshops in the use of the cookers. You can learn more on the SCI website (**www.solarcookersinternational.org**). Consider showing your family or group the pages that offer multiple solar oven designs, recipes for solar cooking, and reports from localities where the move to solar cooking has improved families' health and well-being.

The Project. Experience "green energy" hands-on to practice respect for our interdependent web of life (seventh UU Principle) and to engage the spirit of our fourth UU Principle, a free, responsible search for truth and meaning.

Gather at the worktable you have prepared for building a solar oven. Explain that solar oven cooking is better for the earth than using electrical appliances because it neither uses fossil fuels nor creates pollution. Challenge your family or group to try solar cooking, and then evaluate its pros and cons as compared with your usual indoor methods.

On the pizza box top, use a ruler and a marker to draw lines parallel to three sides of the box, one inch in from each edge. Cut along the three lines to make a flap in the pizza box lid. Fold the flap up so it stands when the box lid is closed.

Cut aluminum foil to cover the inner side of the flap. Glue the aluminum foil to the inner side of the flap, shiny side out.

Use two sheets of clear plastic wrap to create an airtight window for sunlight to enter the box. Do this by opening the box and taping one sheet of plastic wrap across the inside of the opening you made when you cut the flap in the lid. Then close the box and tape the second sheet of plastic wrap across the same opening, on the outside. Tape very securely to seal out air.

Glue aluminum foil to the inside bottom of your box. Cover the aluminum foil with black construction paper (black absorbs heat). The black surface is where you will place food to cook.

Outside in a sunny spot, adjust the flap so the most sunlight possible hits the aluminum foil and reflects onto the plastic-covered window. Prop the flap where you want it, using a straw, wooden spoon, or stick. To tilt the box, place a rolled towel under it. You can preheat the oven as high as 200 degrees Fahrenheit by setting it in direct sunlight for 30 minutes.

Place food items on a tin or glass plate and set the plate in the oven. Once food is cooked, lift the lid of the pizza box and use oven mitts to lift the dish out.

After. Point out that every time we use a microwave, electric, or gas oven, we consume the earth's fossil fuel resources and make pollution that affects people all over the world. Because we use science and reason to help us right wrongs and better our world (our fourth Principle), we know that using a solar oven instead is good for the earth. How successful was today's effort? Can solar cooking be part of your daily routine? What would you lose? What would you gain? Affirm our UU seventh Principle, the interconnection of all life on our planet, by discussing realistic steps your family can take to rely less on appliances in preparing your food. What about helping others realize the benefits of solar cooking? Your family or group may wish to help bring solar cooking technology to people whose everyday lives it can improve. Plan a fundraising event for one of SCI's partner organizations, where you will demonstrate solar cooking with a sale of s'mores.

From *World of Wonder* Session 13 (Green Energy), Tapestry of Faith for grades K/1

9. The Power of Listening

UU Principles 1, 2, 3

Short-term / All ages / ¢

The first Unitarian Universalist Principle affirms the inherent worth and dignity of each person. The second Principle promotes justice, equity, and compassion in human relations, and the third says we support one another's spiritual growth. Listening can be an act of faith that expresses all of these Principles.

Play a game that invites each member to pay extremely close attention to the rest of the group, sharing their voice only when it will not interrupt someone else. With everyone standing in a circle, individuals call out sequential numbers. For instance, Alyssa starts with "one," Kyle says "two," Nara says "three," and so on. Any time a person speaks over another, the count starts over. You must listen carefully to sense when there is empty space into which you can speak. Try to count to ten in this fashion. If you accomplish this goal, try the game again with everyone closing or covering their eyes. Make sure you talk afterward about the game. Was it easy or hard? Why? What about this game might you remember next time you are talking with a group of your friends? How might the world become peaceful and fair if politicians, pundits, and leaders were required to play this game before every public discussion?

From *Sing to the Power* Session 8 (The Power of Listening), Tapestry of Faith for grades 4/5

10. Family Covenant

UU Principles 1, 2, 5

Long-term / Ages 6 and up / ¢

"A covenant . . . calls for a level of trust, courage and sacrifice that needs to be nurtured, renewed and affirmed on a regular basis. . . . Abiding in covenant is an art form. A mutual creation."

—Rev. Lisa Ward

You will need:

- Paper and pencils

Before. Unitarian Universalist groups often make a covenant—a set of mutually agreed promises as to how the individuals will be together. For example, the seven UU Principles are a covenant between the member congregations of the Unitarian Universalist Association. A covenant helps ensure that each person can expect to be treated fairly and considerately and that, in turn, each knows how they must behave to keep their covenant with the group. Whether or not you have articulated them, various promises form the basis of your relationships in your family, your household, or in any close group. Give some thought to the covenants that already exist in your family or group. For example, accepting the responsibility to parent a child, you have made a set of deep promises that you act on every day. Beyond feeding, clothing, and sheltering your child, the love, protection, and guidance you provide fulfill a covenant. Take the time to identify for yourself the covenants that support the relationships in your family or group. What promises do children make? What promises do adults make?

The Project. Making a family covenant together is a beautiful way to honor the inherent worth and dignity of each family member; affirm the justice, equity, and compassion we wish for in our relationships; and practice our fifth Principle, democratic process skills. Make time after a shared meal or take an hour during a quiet evening or weekend for a family (or group) covenant meeting. Explain that a covenant is a set of promises between people in a relationship or a group, such as a family. As examples, share the existing covenants you identified beforehand. Who can think of others? Engage children to explore how family covenants are a two-way street. Your child can understand that respect, for example, goes both ways; unpack specific behaviors with which a child, a youth, or an adult in the family can demonstrate respect.

You might covenant to treat certain times, such as a family meal, in a special way so that nothing outside interferes with your time together. Engage your child as a willing participant in an agreement to turn off electronics or not answer phones at these times.

Take notes on everyone's contributions. Invite everyone to suggest changes as promises emerge. Then ask for a consensus agreement on a final covenant.

After. Post the covenant in a shared family or group space. You may like to express your family's covenant before shared meals as part of prayer or thanksgiving and/or lighting a chalice or candles or at the start of family meetings. Point out, now and then, the instances when you notice someone keeping a covenant. Return to your covenant during family disagreements or whenever group decisions need to be made.

From *Wonderful Welcome* Session 2 (The Gift of Covenant), Tapestry of Faith for grades K/1

11. A Taste of Ethics

UU Principles 4, 7

Short-term / All ages / $

You will need:

- Two packages of ice cream (or another food)
- Bowls, spoons, serving spoons, and napkins
- Writing paper and pencils/pens
- Money for a household grocery shopping trip

Before. Food shopping in our society offers myriad choices. For some consumers, the choices are simple. Avoiding certain ingredients has life-or-death importance for some. By necessity, availability and price matter the most to others. But if you have a generous grocery budget, you can consider multiple factors, such as taste preferences, a familiar brand, or the fun of trying a new brand or a new store. When people make food choices based on their values and beliefs, they are engaging in "ethical eating." Yet ethics are a very personal matter, so no one can define the rules of ethical eating for anyone else. Food shoppers wishing to "eat in faith" might focus on a food manufacturer's labor practices, the ingredients and additives in the food, or the treatment of animals used to make the food. For example, one ethical eater might spend extra to import coffee beans directly from a Kenyan farmers' cooperative. Another ethical eater might prefer to support a local independent grocery

28

store and buy whatever coffee it has on its shelves. Think about the following: When have you expressed your values or ethics through the food you chose to buy? Do you believe some food choices have more virtue than others? Familiarize yourself with issues and questions related to ethical eating. In 2011, the Unitarian Universalist Association adopted "Ethical Eating: Food and Environmental Justice" as a UUA Statement of Conscience. Find resources for study at **www.uua.org/environment/eating**.

Now prepare to lead your family or group into a "free and responsible search for meaning," a fourth Principle exploration of what *ethical eating* means to each of them and how they might practice it. Buy two different brands of a food everyone generally likes, such as vanilla ice cream. Choose one brand with features some people consider ethical—such as all-natural or all-organic ingredients and a fair-trade label, or made locally, thereby reducing carbon emissions associated by trucking in food—and another brand that does not. Prepare two samples for everyone, making sure you know but others do not know which is which; you might put stickers on the bottom of one set of bowls or use different color bowls.

The Project. Offer everyone "a taste of ethics" and invite them to sample the two brands. Ask: Does one taste better than the other? Keep score or write comments as people compare the ice creams. Then reveal which is which.

Now ask: Which one better expresses your values and beliefs? Explain that ethical eating means making food choices based on your values and beliefs. For example, someone might buy only foods grown or made locally to protest the pollution made by trucks, airplanes, and trains that transport food from far away. There is no single rule book for ethical eating, as we each have our own values and beliefs and may choose to express them in different ways. Offer and ask for more examples until contradictory ones surface. (Is it ethical to eat a food that has been transported to our grocery store from a farm 3,000 miles away, in a truck or airplane using huge amounts of fossil fuel? What if that food is, in fact, cheaper than a locally produced alternative, and buying it saves you a few dollars you can then donate to help people in your community heat their homes or purchase the groceries they need?)

Say that good people disagree about the ethics of eating. Some people feel strongly about organic foods and/or about banning meat from their diets. Other people say that not everyone has the financial resources to buy organic food. Point out that our position in the food chain dictates that we must kill something—animal or plant—to eat, or we will die. Unitarian Universalist congregations have members and friends with many different beliefs about food.

What ethical eating decisions does your family make about food? Which values are the decisions based on? Do any two people have different values that lead them to a conflict about whether the family should buy a particular food? See if you can come up with one ethical eating rule that reflects everyone's individual values and concerns.

After. Make a grocery shopping list together for your household. Talk about the ethical choices each food item presents. Then take an ethical food shopping trip. This might mean a trip to a farmers' market or a store that offers local organic produce. It might mean visiting a supermarket for bulk amounts of nonperishables to donate to a food pantry. It could mean shopping at a store whose labor practices you approve of. As you shop, read item labels so your choices can be well-informed.

From *Amazing Grace* Session 4 (Telling Right from Wrong), Tapestry of Faith for grade 6

12. Plant a Hope Garden

UU Principles 3, 7

Long-term / All ages / $

Planting a garden is an act of hope. Gardeners plant with faith that their efforts will yield new life. Rather than expecting to enjoy the garden in its full-grown beauty immediately, those who plant do it for the future and for the good of the environment. Decide where to plant the garden. A window box or even an indoor planter can host a fine garden if you lack outdoor space or favorable weather. Engage everyone in preparing the garden, with roles suited to ages, abilities, and interests. Give everyone a chance to choose seeds or seedlings. Have someone make and someone else decorate a sign (for example, "Welcome to the Miller Family's Hope Garden"). When you are ready to plant seeds or seedlings, a ritual or ceremony can establish the garden as a way you support one another's need for hope. Encourage each individual to share something for which they hope, and give each person a chance to plant something. Leave room in the garden to plant future hopes. You might add a seed or seedling to demonstrate hope for the new relationship when someone joins your family through birth, adoption, or marriage. Plant a hope for a good experience at a new job or school, for the successful addition of a new family pet, or for peace. Families that experience a death might plant new life to symbolize the hope their loved one gave to the world. Arrange how you will share the ongoing care and maintenance of your hope garden.

From *A Place of Wholeness* Workshop 5 (Hope), Tapestry of Faith for high school youth

PROJECTS

Make a Difference Locally

MAKE A DIFFERENCE LOCALLY

13. A Voice for Children

UU Principles 1, 2, 6

Short-term / Age 6 and up / $$

You will need:

- Games, craft supplies, and/or food to share with children who do not currently have homes

Before. Contact a shelter for homeless families or another agency that houses children for long-term care (such as the Ronald McDonald House), and ask about the children's needs. Offer to provide a pizza, game, and/or crafts party, or arrange to bring for each child a special book, toy, or game they may keep. Make sure you are permitted to spend time in direct contact with clients. Clarify any age and other restrictions for visitors/volunteers. If you plan to bring food, find out what you're allowed to bring.

The Project. When a family is homeless, children may not know where they are going to sleep each night. They have little control over how and where they spend their free time and little say about what personal belongings they can have. Affirm the inherent worth and dignity of children without a permanent home by providing an event and/or a gift especially for them. To engage the young people in your family or group, ask them to imagine they must leave their home to live someplace else and can bring only one personal item along. What would they take? Help them think of an item a child might like to have that is small and easy to carry and may help them feel a sense of home. Then find, make, or buy gifts for the children who are homeless. If you will provide a game night or entertainment, young people are likely to have suggestions that the children you are visiting will enjoy.

After. Invite everyone to share something that made them worried or sad during the visit. Then ask volunteers to share something that made them hopeful or happy. Do you think your visit made a difference to the children you visited and their families? How? Why? When someone's biggest need is for a home, it might seem there is nothing we can do to help. But is that true? What other needs might they have that you may be able to help meet? Ask how this activity shows a way to live our Principles. Can paying attention to an individual child and having fun together demonstrate what we believe?

From *Love Surrounds Us* Session 10 (Our Words Matter), Tapestry of Faith for grades K/1

14. Take Your Child to Vote

UU Principles 1, 5

Short-term / All ages / ¢

Our first Unitarian Universalist Principle says that each person is important, and our fifth Principle says that we each should have a voice in matters that concern us. Further, the fifth Principle proclaims our right of conscience and promotes the use of the democratic process. To vote is a Unitarian Universalist act of faith.

One idea that has caught on is a Take Your Child to Vote day. At election time, consider the words of Scott Eliot, a reporter for *Daily News* of Dayton, Ohio, in a piece published on Tuesday, November 7, 2006 (Election Day):

> There's two things I hope you'll do today. The first thing is I hope you vote. The second is I hope you'll take your children with you to the polls, let them watch while you vote and talk to them about who you're voting for and why. . . . Think of it as a one-on-one civics lesson. It's really our best hope for intelligent, engaged citizens in the future, that they learn from adults around them that political participation is an important duty, a thoughtful exercise and that it actually can be exciting and fun.

If you do not want to wait for a public vote, bring children to a decision-making session of your faith community or a local civic governing body. If possible, arrange for children to help collect ballots or count hands in a vote. Afterward, discuss the issues that arose and how they were decided. Help a child articulate the process they observed—a ballot vote, a show of hands, consensus—and identify what made it democratic. Share opinions on how well the democratic process worked. Did it help the group make their decisions? Reach their larger, shared goals? What about the people who lost a vote or compromised so the group could reach consensus? When a democratic process has winners and losers, is it still fair?

Try using a democratic process as a family to make age-appropriate decisions together, such as what to eat for dinner, what movie to watch, or where to go on a weekend outing.

The PBS Kids website has fun, educational interactive pages in a section called the "Democracy Project" (**http://pbskids.org/ democracy/**). Learn about times in U.S. history when one vote has made a difference. Young users can cast a vote about current issues on the website.

Some children enact mock elections in their schools or get to vote for student representatives. Encourage them to bring their UU values to the polls. Ask, "Did your faith or UU values help you decide how to vote?"

From *Toolbox of Faith* Session 7 (Democratic Process), Tapestry of Faith for grades 4/5

15. Welcome Kits

UU Principles 1, 2, 3

Short-term / Ages 6 and up / $

Making a welcome kit for someone in new surroundings is an empathetic thing to do. When you reach out to include someone else in your community, you affirm their inherent worth and dignity and help create the just, equitable, and compassionate human relations our second Unitarian Universalist Principle points us toward. A welcome kit shows you are ready to accept a new member and to help them grow.

Invite your family or group to participate by talking together about times when each of you has been a newcomer, such as to your neighborhood, this country, or a new school, job, or team. What was it like to be new? What made you feel welcome? How could someone have reached out to you to make being a newcomer easier?

Decide together whom you would like to present with a welcome kit. For a new student in someone's school, you might include a map of the school, a welcome card signed by other students, and a folder or pencil with the school name printed on it. The parents of a new classmate or teammate might appreciate contact information for the adults in your family.

Has a new family moved into your neighborhood? A welcome kit might include information on local businesses, the dates of upcoming meetings of the neighborhood association, flyers about neighborhood festivals or events, and an invitation to dinner. Assemble the welcome kit together and deliver it together too.

From *Heeding the Call* Workshop 4 (The Call for Empathy), Tapestry of Faith for junior high school

16. Box House for Homelessness Awareness

UU Principles 1, 2, 6

Long-term / Age 10 and up / ¢

You will need:

- A large cardboard box, like a refrigerator box
- A utility knife
- Large sheets of drawing paper, markers, and tape or glue sticks
- A pocket folder and access to a copy machine

Before. Research homelessness in your area—the number of people without homes, the percentage of homeless people receiving housing services, how many schoolchildren are homeless, how many families have inadequate shelter. Prepare a fact sheet or gather URLs to help others in your family or group do some research on their own. Decide where to display the box house—at a public park, in front of your home, at your congregation, outside a popular store or community center—and for how long. Seek permission if needed.

The Project. Cut a door in the cardboard box to suggest a house. Decorate the outside with local homelessness statistics from your research. Add a message such as, "What if this were all the home you had?" to draw attention to the needs of people who are homeless. Copy your fact sheet to leave in a pocket folder outside the box house. Use the fact sheet to suggest ways people can help and to provide contact information for local homelessness-focused agencies or organizations that can use volunteers or donations.

After. Visit the box house where it is displayed and replenish fact sheets if needed. Talk about the ways having a home supports someone's inherent worth and dignity. For example, losing one's home can mean losing shelter, privacy, family support, and much more. Consider inviting others to join you in a fundraiser that many Unitarian Universalist youth groups and congregations have done: Make a few more box houses and invite people to sponsor individuals to sleep outdoors in a box house. Donate proceeds to a homeless shelter or service organization as an expression of justice, equity, and compassion in human relations—the values lifted up by our second Principle.

From *Love Connects Us* Session 15 (All Work Together), Tapestry of Faith for grades 4/5

MAKE A DIFFERENCE LOCALLY

17. Changing the Rules

UU Principles 1, 2, 5

Short-term / Age 6 and up / ¢

You will need:

- The text of a law or rule you wish to consider
- Letter-writing supplies: paper, pens, envelopes, and stamps

Before. Select a local, state, or national law or rule whose fairness is worthy of debate. Identify officials to whom you might propose a change to the law or rule. Obtain their contact information.

You might choose a rule that affects members of your family or group, such as a school dress code. For example, at your child's school, can a person of any gender wear any jewelry they wish to? Are tee-shirt slogans restricted?

You might propose or lobby for a law that affirms Unitarian Universalist Principles by striving for equality. For example, does your state need a new law to protect everyone's access to fair wages or high-quality education, housing, or health care? Do you live in a state where equal marriage for same-sex couples is not guaranteed by law? You are sure to find interesting issues in the news. Engage all ages to look for an issue to act on.

The Project. Discuss the law or rule and ways you would propose to change it. Be sure to think through the consequences of what you will suggest. If you oppose a rule, consider what might happen without it. If you support a rule, what might be the consequences of keeping or enacting it? Measure your proposal against our first and second Principles: Would the change you seek promote "justice, equity, and compassion in human relations" or restore respect for "the inherent worth and dignity of every person"?

Come to consensus. Then write a group letter to somebody with power to change the rule or law. Make sure to mention that you speak as people of faith. Share your idea with the public too. Where can you display a poster to call attention to the rule and the change you propose? Decide who your audience is and what you want to communicate. Design, make, and display posters.

Alternately, start a petition that people who support your idea can sign in person, or post one on a social networking site such as Change.org or Tumblr.

After. Point out that making these efforts is a beautiful way to follow our consciences and use our right of free speech. When we speak up for a change we believe in, we demonstrate our fifth Unitarian Universalist Principle, that everyone should have a say in matters that concern them. If needed, follow up with the recipient(s) of your letter. Share any responses to the letter or posters with your family or group. You may find yourselves leading a movement. How far do you wish to take "use of the democratic process"—our fifth Principle—with regard to this rule or law? What are your next steps? Changing a rule can take a long time, even when a majority of decision makers or voters like your idea. Be sure to name your successes in this work while you are waiting for change to come, and even if your proposal fails. Discuss how it feels to act as an agent of change in the world.

From *Amazing Grace* Session 11 (Rules, Rules, Rules), Tapestry of Faith for grade 6

18. Get There by People Power

UU Principles 3, 7

Short-term / All ages / ¢

You will need:

- Poster board, markers, and tape
- Water and snacks for those who arrive via "people power"

Before. Choose a recurring community event you regularly participate in, such as attending Sunday worship. Consult your calendars for a date when everyone in the family can make the excursion together and take the extra time to get there by "people power" rather than by car. Plan how you will promote Get There by People Power Day to others. If your destination will be your UU congregation, plan to display posters there. Ask worship leaders and your newsletter editor to promote the people power plan several weeks ahead.

The Project. A Get There by People Power Day benefits our ecosystem, fosters connections between individuals and our natural environment, and unites in common purpose a family or community that conserves fossil fuel together. People power can include sharing rides, traveling together by public transportation, or literally using human energy to walk or bicycle.

After. Compare stories of everyone's travel to the same destination. Which modes took longer or were more inconvenient than the usual mode of travel? Which were more pleasant or fun? Did people power actually shorten anyone's trip? Point out that Get There by People Power Day is a way to take faithful action that is particularly expressive of our seventh Principle. The broader the participation you can inspire, the more strongly the community encourages one another's spiritual growth through this project, serving our third Principle too. Now that you have tried it once, plan to seek more participants and schedule a day to try it again. Consider making people power travel part of your regular routine.

From *Faithful Journeys* Session 14 (Honor Life), Tapestry of Faith for grades 2/3

19. Care Packages for Any Soldier

UU Principles 2, 6

Short- or long-term / All ages / $$

Unitarian Universalism seeks peace, and our movement has a strong tradition of nonviolent opposition to war. Therefore, UUs sometimes struggle with the conflict between deploring war and supporting the soldiers who risk their lives to protect and defend the United States, its citizens, and our democratic way of life. Even if you abhor the military or the ways our government deploys its force—in fact, especially if you have such feelings—you can make a strong authentic statement of faith by easing the hardship of a U.S. soldier serving overseas. Any Soldier is an internet-based organization founded in 2003 by the parents of Brian Horn, who served as an Army sergeant in Iraq and Afghanistan. Through its website, **www.anysoldier.com**, active duty members of the Armed Services volunteer as contacts so civilians can send letters and care packages to Air Force, Army, Coast Guard, Marine, or Navy posts and be assured their package will be delivered to a soldier who has asked for this support. The website describes items appropriate to send and gives full instructions for packing and addressing care packages. Visit the website together. Talk about why Brian Horn's parents started Any Soldier. Write a letter to an anonymous soldier and choose items for a care package together. Lift up your action as an expression of our second and sixth UU Principles, which affirm us to demonstrate compassion and justice to move humanity toward a peaceful and fair world community. Be ready to lead a frank, age-appropriate conversation with these questions: How can helping a soldier show that we prefer peace to war? Why would someone who dislikes war decide to be a soldier? Does someone who fights as a soldier deserve our compassion and friendship?

Explain that for many young people, a job in the military offers pay, training opportunities, and assistance for college tuition that they may not find anyplace else. Say that while soldiers must be prepared for violent conflict when they are sent overseas, they also often help people in the countries where they serve by building, teaching, and getting to know individuals and communities to better understand all sides of the conflict. Point out that even when our government deploys soldiers, its objective may be peace, just like ours. If we disagree with how our government uses the people in our Armed Services and deplore the danger and hardship all soldiers face, we can still acknowledge that sometimes governments use war as a way to resolve conflict so there can be peace. Is war ever worth it? How can we support soldiers with compassion even while we wish for a world without soldiers, a world at peace?

From *Moral Tales* Session 8 (Do Unto Others), Tapestry of Faith for grades 2/3

20. Saving Animals

UU Principles 2, 7

Long-term / Ages 10 and up / ¢

For Unitarian Universalists, to help animals is to honor the seventh Principle, which asks us to respect the "interdependent web of all existence of which we are a part." This means all living things, not just people. Also, our second Principle's call for justice and compassion in human relations surely embraces the pets, livestock, and wild species affected by human activity. If working to save and protect animals appeals to you, connect with an organization that can use your help. Be ready to recognize and name this work as a calling—a faith-directed choice.

Contact animal shelters, the animal control officer, and animal rescue and advocacy groups in your community. Ask them:

- What problems do you try to solve?
- What do the animals need?
- How can volunteers help?

Describe the ages and interests of the young people you want to engage. Typical projects might be donating towels and blankets, delivering food or medicine donated by veterinary clinics or pet supply stores, and helping to publicize a pet adoption event or a spay/neuter clinic. You might offer to decorate a waiting room or office area. Perhaps you can persuade a veterinarian to donate free-visit vouchers to anyone adopting from a shelter. Volunteering on-site to visit shelter cats or walk shelter dogs, clean cages, staff a front desk, or feed the animals may be open only to older youth, or may require some training and/or the supervision of a parent. If a young person is ready and willing to make the commitment, think of ways other family members can support them.

If the family is willing to make a larger commitment, consider becoming foster parents to homeless pets. Healthy Pets has an article on becoming a foster parent at **http://healthypets.mercola .com/sites/healthypets/archive/2012/04/18/pet-fostering.aspx**. You can also find many useful resources at **www.petfoster.org**.

From *Amazing Grace* Session 7 (The Second U), Tapestry of Faith for grade 6

21. Making Blankets for People Who Are Homeless

UU Principles 1, 2, 6

Short-term / Ages 6 and up / $$

You will need:

- Large pieces of fleece fabric
- Scissors

Before. Identify a homeless shelter in your area where you can donate the blankets you make. Find out the shelter's specifications for materials to use and the size of the blankets. Ask when and to whom you can deliver finished blankets. If possible, arrange to talk with shelter staff on-site about how the blankets will be distributed and why they will be useful to people who are homeless.

Purchase fleece fabric. You will need two pieces that are 39" x 74" each for a blanket that just covers a twin-size bed. Find a story to read aloud and discuss together before or during a blanket-knotting session that focuses on a situation of homelessness. Look for a story that establishes that everyone deserves a home (our first Principle of inherent worth and dignity), invites discussion of what someone might need who finds themselves without one (our second Principle of love and justice), and demonstrates a way we can help one another when someone is without a home (our seventh Principle of interconnectedness). You might share a story that emphasizes caring and loyalty, such as "Ruth and Naomi," based on the biblical story. Younger children may respond to "Owen and Mzee," a true story about a baby hippo who bonded with an aged tortoise when he was relocated to an animal sanctuary. These two stories, from the Tapestry of Faith curriculum *Creating Home*, for grades K/1, appear on pages 52 and 53, respectively.

The Project. Help provide for some of the needs of people who are homeless by making cozy, lightweight, washable knotted blankets out of fleece. Explain that while every person needs and deserves a safe home, some people do not have a place to live or their own bed to sleep in. A homeless shelter is a warm, safe place where people without a home can sleep overnight. Explain that few shelters are big enough to always have a bed for all who need one. On some nights, some people need to look for a safe, comfortable place to sleep outdoors. A blanket made of fleece fabric is lightweight to carry, warm, and washable. It is a practical, useful item a homeless shelter can give to any person to whom they are unable to offer a bed. Invite everyone to knot a blanket to make someone's time without a home more comfortable and to show them they are not alone—that others care.

To make a blanket:

1. Fold a sheet of fleece fabric in half. Cut a 2" square from the two corners that are not folded.
2. Cut 2" of long fringe around the perimeter of the fabric, along the three open edges, not the folded edge. Make each fringe about 3/4" wide.
3. Unfold the fabric and lay it flat. Starting at a corner, tie pairs of fringe strips in square knots (right over left, then left over right).
4. Pull knots gently to tighten. If you end up with an odd number of fringes, include three in the last knot.

After. Take the finished blankets to the shelter you have selected and talk with shelter staff as you have arranged to do. Afterward, go together to a place where you can respond together to your experience. Invite everyone to share how making the blankets and visiting the shelter made them feel. Point out that because we believe each person has inherent worth and dignity, we also believe each person has the right to a warm, safe place to sleep every night. Affirm that it is worthwhile to do one thing to make a person's situation a little better, even though we may feel sad that we cannot do more.

From *Creating Home* Session 7 (Book of Ruth), Tapestry of Faith for grades K/1

Story: Ruth and Naomi

Adapted from Hebrew scripture

Once, long ago, in the city of Bethlehem, in the land of Judah, there lived a man named Elimelech. Elimelech was married to Naomi and they had two sons, Klion and Mahlon. The time came when a great famine struck Bethlehem and the farmers could not produce enough food for everyone in the city. Elimelech was no longer able to provide for his family, so he decided they would move to another city, Moab.

Several years later, Elimelech died. His wife, Naomi, was getting older, too. Her sons and their wives, Orpah and Ruth, helped to care for her but, sadly, after living in Moab for ten years, Naomi's sons both died, too.

When Naomi heard that the famine in Bethlehem was over, she wanted to leave Moab and return home. Her daughters-in-law, Orpah and Ruth, walked along with her toward Bethlehem to keep her company on the journey. When they were almost there, Naomi turned to her daughters-in-law. She blessed them for looking after her and for having been good wives to her two sons. She praised them for being loyal. "Return to Moab, to your families," Naomi said.

At first, neither woman wanted to leave Naomi. Then Orpah turned back and went home. But Ruth would not leave Naomi. She said, "Where you go I will go, and where you stay I will stay. Your people shall be my people and your god my god. Nothing will ever separate us." Naomi saw that Ruth was determined. So the two women returned to Naomi's hometown. They found a place to live in Bethlehem, but although the famine had ended—in fact, it was harvest time—the two women had no food.

One day, Ruth and Naomi saw some women walking behind the men harvesting barley, picking up the stray stalks the men left behind. Ruth went to a neighbor's farm and started doing the same. The farmer who owned those fields was named Boaz. He saw Ruth collecting stalks of barley on his farm and asked his workers who she was. They told him about Naomi's return and that this woman, Ruth, was the dutiful, loving daughter-in-law from Moab, who had come back to Bethlehem with Naomi to live with her and take care of her.

When Boaz learned how devoted Ruth was to her mother-in-law Naomi, he thought, "Surely God looks kindly on Ruth." He instructed his workers to leave extra barley unpicked in the fields to make sure Ruth could gather enough to eat. Ruth ground the barley and used it to bake bread for herself and Naomi.

Boaz could see Ruth's loyalty in the way she took care of Naomi. Boaz felt responsible to help, too, and he enjoyed being with Ruth, so he asked her to marry him, and she said "yes." After Boaz and Ruth married, Naomi lived with them. When Boaz and Ruth had a little son, Naomi helped to take care of him, as a grandmother.

Story: Owen and Mzee

Not so long ago, in Kenya, on a peaceful river near the east coast of Africa, a herd of hippopotamuses was surprised by heavy rain. The rain washed them away from their river home toward the Indian Ocean. Then came something worse. A tsunami! In the huge, windy storm the ocean waters became strong.

The hippos were in danger. They had to get back to the shore. But the tsunami made the ocean strong and wild. Most of the hippos did not make it.

When the tsunami came, the people who lived near the ocean were afraid. Neighbors rushed to help rescue fishermen who were out on their boats in the wild ocean. Families ran away from the ocean. They were afraid the water and wind would wreck their homes, and they wanted to get to a safer place as fast as they could. Nobody was thinking about the hippos.

A few days later, the sky was blue again and the Indian Ocean was quiet again. Many homes had been destroyed by water and wind. People began to clean up and fix everything.

On the shore of the ocean, a lone survivor needed help—one of the hippos, a baby. He was the only member of his family left, and he was standing on a reef in the ocean, all alone.

People ran to help rescue the hippo, and many more came to watch. A hippo is very big and heavy, even a baby. And this hippo was also wet, tired, and upset. Would he let the people help him?

[*Ask: How do you think the people could rescue the hippo?*]

Here is what they used: Ropes. Cars. Boats. Fishing nets, huge ones. But the baby hippo was frightened and did not want to come along. He was so large, fast, and slippery, nobody could grab him to bring him to safety. Finally, when the hippo was tangled up in a big fishing net, a strong man named Owen jumped on the hippo and captured him.

[*Ask: What do you think happened next?*]

Kenya has a wildlife refuge where animals that lose their homes in the wild can be safe in surroundings like what they are used to. Paula Kahumbu worked at that wildlife refuge. She came to the ocean to get the baby hippo and bring him to Haller Park, where he would be safe. She brought a veterinarian, Dr. Kashmiri, and an animal caretaker, Stephen Tuei.

With lots of persistence and lots of help, Paula Kahumbu and Stephen Tuei managed to get the baby hippo onto their truck. The people by the ocean who had watched the incredible rescue agreed the baby hippo should be named Owen, after the man who had successfully tackled him. And off they went, to Haller Park.

Baby Owen was confused and scared when they arrived. No one was surprised. After all, the baby hippo had lost his home and his family. But, to everyone's surprise, right away Owen found someone to protect him. Do you think he found a new hippopotamus mother or dad? Not exactly. He ran right over to Mzee [pronounced Muh-ZAY].

Mzee was not a hippo. Mzee was a giant tortoise, a kind of turtle, so big he was almost the same size as Owen. Mzee was 130 years old.

At first Mzee acted puzzled that Owen was following him around and trying to sleep right next to him, just like a baby hippo would do with its hippo mother. Stephen Tuei wondered what was going to happen. After a few days, Mzee did not seem to mind the baby hippo's company. Tortoises and hippos both enjoy going in the water. Owen followed Mzee when he went swimming and tried to share Mzee's food too. Mzee didn't like that so much. But the two stuck together most of every day. Owen became more and more used to his new home in Haller Park. And he always slept right next to Mzee.

22. Luminaria: Shining Our Light for Justice

UU Principles 2, 4, 6

Short-term / Ages 10 and up / $

You will need:

- Paper lunch bags, tea lights, pencils, and scissors
- Sand—enough to fill each paper bag 1/3 full
- Optional: Colored tissue paper and clear tape
- Optional: Copies of *Singing the Living Tradition* (UUA Publication, 1993)
- Optional: Camera

Before. Choose or initiate an evening film screening or a public talk in your community to highlight an individual's actions for justice. Obtain permission to place luminary candles along a walkway to the event or at an entrance. Some biopics to consider for young teens and older are *42* (Jackie Robinson, the first African-American major league baseball player), *The Blind Side* (Leigh Anne Tuohy, a middle-class mother who adopted Michael Oher, an impoverished youth, nurturing his rise as a National Football League star), *Erin Brockovich* (an American citizen who led the fight to bring a polluting California power company to justice), *Gandhi* (Mohandas K. Gandhi, leader of India's nonviolent overthrow of British rule), *Gorillas in the Mist* (Dian Fossey, an American zoologist who worked to protect primates of Africa's Virunga Mountains), *Mandela: Long Walk to Freedom* (Nelson Mandela, the first democratically elected president of South Africa), *Milk* (Harvey Milk, an American gay activist), *Schindler's List* (Oskar Schindler, a German businessman who helped Jews escape the Holocaust), and *Two Who Dared* (Martha and Rev. Waitstill Sharp, American Unitarians who rescued intellectuals and Jewish children from World War II Europe).

The Project. Make luminaria to symbolize the potential for each one of us to shine our light for justice. Explain the event to which the luminaria will light the way. Describe the justice cause that inspired the film's central character or the speaker you will hear, and share what you know about the actions that person took for justice. Now help one another think of ways you share, or can share, your individual qualities or skills to serve a justice cause. Interpret "justice cause" broadly. A child may have stood up to a bully, shared food with someone who had none, or admitted to a teacher that they were responsible for a misdeed at school. Affirm that every single light for justice matters. Encourage each person to illustrate the justice light they shine by drawing on or cutting into a paper bag. Make cuts in the top third of the bag only! Help young children draw their ideas, then cut designs into their paper bags around their artwork. For a stained glass effect, cover the cutout shapes by taping colored tissue paper to the inside of the bag. Fill each paper bag 1/3 full with sand and place a tea light in the sand.

After. Bring your luminaria to the event and light them. Notice how combining them makes a bigger light. If appropriate, lead a community sing of "This Little Light of Mine," hymn 118 in the Unitarian Universalist hymnbook, *Singing the Living Tradition*. Take photographs. After the event, make a photo poster or scrapbook. Add your reflections about the event. Do you think the luminaria helped to highlight the justice-seeking mission of the event? If so, why? Why do you think justice and lights seem to go well together?

From *Toolbox of Faith* Session 14 (Justice), Tapestry of Faith for grades 4/5

23. Dignity Behind Bars

UU Principles 1, 6

Short- or long-term / Ages 10 and up / ¢

The statistics of the current United States prison population are staggering. More than two million people are in prison, which is more than any country in recorded history has ever had in prison at one time. The fact that most inmates are people of color and/or people coming from poverty only legitimizes the claim that our justice system is tragically flawed by the injustices of racism and classism. Doing a project that nurtures the dignity and self-respect of a prisoner is a way to live our first Unitarian Universalist Principle; some UU congregations have prison ministries that coordinate such projects.

The prison ministry of the Church of the Larger Fellowship, an online congregation of Unitarian Universalists, helps individuals and families to correspond confidentially (only first names are used) with people currently in prison in the United States. Children and youth can participate with a parent or guardian over twenty-one who commits to the project. Plan to correspond for a minimum of six months.

Another possibility is to help the United First Parish Church in Quincy, Massachusetts, in its partnership with the Prison Book

Program. The congregation has given the program office and storage space since 2004 and, at this writing, seeks donations to purchase 1,000 dictionaries at a reduced bulk price to donate to prisoners.

In the Pacific Northwest, Books to Prisoners partners with Left Bank Books in Seattle, Washington, to fill book orders from letters they receive from inmates. Popular requests are dictionaries, thesauruses, African-American history and fiction, Native American studies, legal material, and high school graduate equivalency degree (GED) study materials. Many people incarcerated in our prison system are working to obtain a GED or improve their English skills. Others simply enjoy literature and appreciate good books. Consider donating books to this organization or volunteering to fulfill orders if you live near a local branch.

From *Heeding the Call* Workshop 11 (The Call for Forgiveness), Tapestry of Faith for junior high school

24. UU Bumper Stickers

UU Principles 4, 5

Short-term / All ages / $

You will need:

- Paper and pencils
- Waterproof vinyl sticker paper or sticker paper and acrylic paint
- Bold markers
- Lamination supplies

Before. Obtain supplies from a craft store, from an office supply store, or online. You can purchase sticker paper for fifteen heavyweight bumper stickers for $8 at **www.misterinkjet.com/inkjet-printer-labels.htm.**

The Project. Visit a parking lot that is likely to have many cars with message bumper stickers—for example, a Unitarian Universalist congregation on a Sunday morning. Stay in a group for safety as you examine the bumper stickers on a fourth UU Principle tour—a "free and responsible search for meaning." Talk about which ones you like, and why. Make notes or sketches of messages you agree with, disagree with, or find interesting. Then go to an indoor work space and make your own bumper stickers. If anyone seems stuck, suggest some local or global issues or causes until you find one they care about.

After. Once bumper stickers are complete, laminate them, add vinyl covering, or spray with clear acrylic paint. Take the time to view and respond to one another's bumper stickers. Which grab your attention? Which surprise you or make you laugh? If one has a message you disagree with or had never thought about, does it convince you? Why? Can one bumper sticker change someone's mind or actions and help make the world that much better? Unitarian Universalists believe that it can. Invite each car owner in the group to choose a bumper sticker, or several, to display on their vehicle. Invite ideas for other places to place bumper stickers, like on bikes or notebook covers. Your group could make dozens of bumper stickers to donate to raise funds for a cause. When you use bumper stickers to share a message of love, peace, or justice, you affirm our fifth Unitarian Universalist Principle, the right of conscience and the practice of free expression in our democratic society.

Extend the activity by asking group or family members if they are always mindful of messages they proclaim to the world. Do they own tee-shirts with messages that do not truly reflect their beliefs and values? What about buttons?

The Standing on the Side of Love campaign is a way many UUs and UU congregations and communities engage in justice activities. Find out more about it at **http://standingonthesideoflove .org/**. You can order tee-shirts, buttons, and bumper stickers with the slogan from the UUA Bookstore at **www.uuabookstore.org**. But be prepared! If someone asks you what your bumper sticker means, how will you answer? Practice your answers together before displaying the slogan.

From *Amazing Grace* Session 5 (Unitarian Universalism), Tapestry of Faith for grade 6

PROJECTS

Citizens of the World

25. Toilet Tax

UU Principles 1, 6, 7

Short-term / All ages / $

You will need:

- Information about the need for sanitation and clean, safe water in parts of Africa, Asia, and Central America
- Boxes or jars for collecting money

Before. Gather stories and statistics of global inequities related to sanitation, clean water, and public health. A good source is the U.S. website of Water Aid, a nonprofit international organization that funds and implements local water and sanitation projects in developing nations, **www.wateraidamerica.org**. Many smaller organizations also seek funds for local sanitation and clean water projects, like **www.dropinthebucket.org** (Uganda), **www.waves forwater.org** (Brazil, Ethiopia, Haiti, Indonesia, and more), and Middle East Children's Alliance's Maia Project, **www.mecafor-peace.org** (Gaza). Decide where to donate the funds you will raise.

Schedule a day or a week to collect "toilet taxes": money donated by individuals every time they use the toilet. Join the international effort on November 19, the official United Nations World Toilet Day (**www.un.org/en/events/toiletday/**). Or plan to collect a toilet tax at a holiday celebration, local carnival, or other event where you are likely to attract attention and donations. Choose a location and, if needed, obtain permission to collect a voluntary toilet tax outside bathrooms.

The Project. Raise awareness and funds to improve people's access to sanitation and clean water in developing nations.

Spend some time talking about the statistics and stories you have found online. Point out that while a donation is voluntary, a tax is an obligation. Our seventh Principle affirms our place on earth's interconnected web, and our sixth Principle affirms goals of peace and justice for everyone in the world. We and the people across the world who lack water or bathrooms belong to a single world community. We are obligated to them. Reflect together on how a safe, private place to defecate affirms an individual's inherent dignity and self-worth. Discuss what it might be like to live without clean water and sanitation.

Incorporate the most powerful statistics into toilet tax collection posters. Suggested text:

Toilet Tax

Please pay what you can before entering the bathroom. This action is to raise awareness and money to help solve the problem of a lack of sanitation and clean water in much of the world. Your Toilet Tax donation will be sent to WaterAid, an international organization that works with communities in developing nations to bring sanitation and clean water.

Did you know?

- More than 2.5 billion people do not have somewhere safe, private, or hygienic to go to the toilet.
- One gram (.03 ounces) of feces can contain 10 million viruses, one million bacteria, 1,000 parasite cysts, and 100 parasite eggs.

- The simple act of washing hands with soap and water after going to the toilet can reduce diarrheal diseases by over 40%.

  —from WaterAid UK, **www.wateraid.org/uk/get -involved/world-toilet-day**

Make the posters. Display them with collection boxes according to your plan. You may wish to collect the toilet tax in person so you can talk directly to bathroom users about the world's sanitation and clean water inequities, and so you need not leave collection boxes unattended.

After. Follow through by donating toilet tax collections to the organization(s) you chose. Talk about the tangible impact your donation will make. Keep family and community attention on global water justice by sharing photos and reports from your toilet tax collection. Consider more water justice actions you can take to show you care about a fair and peaceful world community (sixth Principle).

From *Gather the Spirit* Session 4 (Conscience Refined), Tapestry of Faith multigenerational program

26. Hunger Games

UU Principles 1, 2, 6

Short-term, can be extended / Ages 6 and up / $

You will need:

• Computer with Internet access

Before. Choose one or more online games to explore world hunger problems, solutions, and actions you can take to help. Preview and play games to decide if they will be appropriate and interesting to all ages in your family or group. Below are a few examples. An Internet search might turn up others, including board games. One such board game is Hunger Cycle (**www.worldvision.org/ resources.nsf/main/edu-2/$file/hunger-cycle.pdf**) offered by World Vision, a Christian organization dedicated to helping children and their families break free from poverty.

Food Force takes players online to Facebook to learn how the United Nations World Food Programme (WFP) supports farming and food distribution to areas where hunger is widespread. Sharing this game with Facebook friends helps fund the WFP's work (**www.gamesforchange.org**).

Free Rice (**www.freerice.com**) is a vocabulary quiz game you can play daily. For each correct answer, website sponsors donate ten grains of rice to WFP for humanitarian aid. Choose "Teaching

Material" from the home page to find a few key world hunger statistics and an interactive five-question quiz.

Darfur is Dying was designed by students at the University of Southern California to simulate refugee survival in a war zone (**www.darfurisdying.com**).

Project. Play one or more interactive games. While playing or immediately after, talk about the game(s): What was it like to play? What was surprising? What was disappointing? What gave you hope? Did the game remind you of any real life experiences? How?

Name ways that long-term hunger can compromise someone's inherent worth and dignity. Could you go to school or do a job without adequate food? How might going without nutritious food during infancy or childhood affect life as an adult? Point out that the food thrown away by people who have plenty could eliminate hunger among people who do not have enough, if only we had a way to distribute the world's food more fairly. If we believe in justice, equity, and compassion (second Principle) and want to build a world community that is fair for everyone (sixth Principle), taking action against world hunger is a good way to show our faith.

After. Follow the links into the WFP web pages to learn ways to support the United Nations WFP relief services. Commit, as a family or group, to an awareness or fundraising action to help mitigate hunger someplace in the world. Sharing one of the WFP games with online contacts is a relatively easy action you can take.

From *Riddle and Mystery* Session 14 (Life as Mystery), Tapestry of Faith for grade 6

27. Audubon Bird Count

UU Principles 4, 7

Short-term, can be extended / All ages / $

You will need:

- Computer with Internet access
- Binoculars, notebooks, and pens

Before. Go to the National Audubon Society website (**www.
audubon.org**) and learn how to participate in the century-old
Christmas Bird Count (CBC) that takes place each year between
December 14 and January 5.

Project. Through the CBC and other bird-monitoring opportunities, such as the Great Backyard Bird Count and Hummingbirds
at Home, the Audubon Society makes it easy for a family and/or
multigenerational group to become citizen scientists together. On
the website, you can locate a local CBC Count Circle, find tips on
bird watching (including how to select and use binoculars), and
register to enter your observations online. Explore the website and
make plans to participate in a local count. If your home is located
in a desirable spot, you may be invited to install a bird feeder and
report on the birds that visit it. The data you gather will help scien-

tists understand the habits and status of bird species. As a citizen scientist, you are living our fourth Principle, "a free and responsible search for truth," as well as our seventh Principle, "respect for the interdependent web."

After. Return to the National Audubon Society website after you have submitted your CBC observations. Spend some time looking at "State of the Birds" and other reports to see how scientists compile and analyze local observation data to document adaptations, declines, and other trends in North American bird populations, and highlight species and habitats at greatest risk. Analyze your own research in the spirit of our fourth Unitarian Universalist Principle: What conclusions can you draw from your data? What might you expect to observe next year? Do your ideas match those of the Audubon scientists, or are yours different? What helpful actions do the data suggest to protect bird wildlife? Commit to at least one.

From *Creating Home* Session 4 (Animal Homes), Tapestry of Faith for grades K/1

28. Carbon Footprint Audit

UU Principles 4, 7

Short-term, can be extended / Age 8 and up / $

Assess the impact your daily life makes on our planet's ecology with an online audit. Many websites allow you to calculate your or your household's carbon footprint. Find free audits suitable for all ages at **www.treeswaterpeople.org**, **www.cooltheworld.com**, and **www.meetthegreens.org** (requires registration and log-in). Compare the results you get from several different online audits. Compare your individual carbon footprints. Family members who drive a car are likely to generate more carbon dioxide than passengers. But is the driver the only one responsible? Maybe family members can forego a few rides and instead walk, ride a bicycle, or consolidate errands into one trip.

Explore a website where you found an informative carbon footprint calculator for suggested lifestyle changes that would be healthier for the planet. Have every person commit to one carbon-reducing change. Work together on weatherizing projects such as installing weather stripping around doors. Acknowledge that we use reason and science (our fourth Principle values) to protect the ecology of our planet (our seventh Principle web of all existence).

From *Sing to the Power* Session 11 (The Power of Action), Tapestry of Faith for grades 4/5

29. Living Simply

UU Principles 1, 6, 7

Long-term / All ages / $

You will need:

- Paper and pencils
- Money collection container

Before. This project engages you directly in redistributing the world's access to food. Money you save through simple living commitments literally feeds someone hungry who is living simply by circumstances rather than by choice. The power of this project lies in creating a caring relationship with specific people you will never meet. Take time to identify a sustainable food or hunger relief organization that documents its impact with stories about real individuals and families. Engage children with the story "The Dog and the Heartless King." Originally a Buddhist story, the version reprinted below is adapted from a telling by Sophia Lyon Fahs and featured in the UUA Tapestry of Faith curriculum *Moral Tales*. In the story, a greedy king hoards food for himself while the populace is hungry. A huge dog is brought to the kingdom, and it barks continuously until all people in the kingdom are adequately fed.

Sum up: This story shows redistribution of wealth as a fair way to solve the problem of hunger.

The Project. Generally speaking, people in the United States have a much higher standard of living than people in many other parts of the world. Everyday items that most people in the U.S. take for granted are considered luxuries by many others. This activity is meant to encourage the spiritual practice of simplicity while making a connection between patterns of consumption and justice. It brings justice from a conceptual realm to the concrete world of everyday actions.

For a period of a week or a month, have each family member give up something that costs money, something they enjoy but that is not necessary for general health and well-being. For example, give up chocolate candy, potato chips, going to the movies, buying toys, cable TV, text messaging, or eating at restaurants. Set aside the money that would have been spent on this item or activity. Donate it to an organization that works for global economic justice, such as the Unitarian Universalist Service Committee (**www.uusc.org**).

After. Can your family commit to continuing the practice of living simply? Ritualize your commitment in a ceremony. Have each person decorate a rock to represent the item or activity they are giving up. Sit in a circle and say something like, "As long as there are people in the world who do not have enough food to eat, clean water to drink, a home to live in, and access to education and medicine, all people must work for justice. In small ways, we can change our lives so that others can create better lives." Have each person put their rock into a decorative container and state, "I will live simply that others may simply live. I promise to give up ___ for one week/ month." If desired, you can allow time for everyone to explain why they have chosen to give up that particular item or activity.

Place the decorative container filled with rocks in a central, visible location in your home. Place a jar or piggy bank near the rocks and use it to collect the money you would have spent on the item or activity you have given up.

At the end of the week or month, gather again to discuss the amount of money you were able to save for donation and each person's experience of giving up an enjoyed activity or item. Have each person light a candle of hope and express a wish or prayer for the people of the world. Consider a commitment to continue to live simply by evaluating future purchases on the basis of whether you really need them. You do not need to deny yourself every luxury item, but this practice will create more intention around your spending habits—and possibly reduce the clutter in your home.

From *Moral Tales* Session 13 (Justice for All), Tapestry of Faith for grades 2/3

Story: The Dog and the Heartless King

Adapted for Tapestry of Faith by Alice Anacheka-Nasemann from "The Heartless King," an Indian folktale adapted by Sophia Fahs in *From Long Ago and Many Lands*, second edition, by Sophia Fahs and Patricia Hoertdoerfer, and illustrated by Cyrus Leroy Baldridge (Boston: Skinner House Books, 1995).

Once upon a time there lived a king who cared for nobody but himself. He had grown rich from the high taxes he had forced his people to pay, while they had become poorer and poorer. He lived in a gorgeous palace, while the poor people who built it for him still lived in thatched huts and tumble-down hovels. The king's table was always heaped with delicious foods, while most of his people had only one plain meal a day, and sometimes not even that. But the heartless king did not care. If he had what he wanted, that was enough for him.

One day a hunter came to the palace gate, intending to teach the heartless king a lesson. The hunter brought with him an enormous dog. The king was fond of hunting and this enormous dog fascinated him. So the hunter and the dog were both welcomed into the palace grounds.

But the enormous dog was no ordinary dog, and her bark was like the roar of thunder. The first time she opened her big mouth and barked, the awful noise shook the walls of the palace and frightened the king and all his courtiers. If the dog had stopped with one or two barks, the matter might have been forgotten.

But again and again her fierce roaring shook the palace and the Earth itself. Before long there was no resting between barks. Nobody in the palace could hear themselves talk. The king was desperate and sent for the hunter. He asked, "Why does your dog make such a deafening noise?"

"The dog is hungry," said the hunter.

Immediately the king ordered that a big plateful of meat be brought. In almost no time at all, the enormous dog licked the plate clean. Then at once she began barking again.

A second plateful of meat was brought. This the dog disposed of just as quickly as the first. Again the dog began barking.

Over and over the plate was filled, and over and over the enormous dog quickly ate the whole plateful and began barking as loudly as ever. The king was angry. He called the hunter and said:

"You and your dog must leave the palace at once. We cannot endure this deafening noise any longer." But the hunter was firm.

"Your Majesty, we have been sent to you by One greater than you are. We are here to stay." The king was frightened. He grasped the arms of his chair and stared at the hunter. The king was not accustomed to having anyone speak to him in this manner.

"Will nothing satisfy the hunger of your enormous dog?" the king said at last.

"Nothing that is easy for you to give," said the hunter. "Your Majesty, there are people in this kingdom who are eating all the food and who are not sharing it with those who do the work in the field to make the food grow. As a result, there are people who are always hungry. This dog feels the hunger of every person in this kingdom who does not have enough food to eat. As long as even one person is hungry, this dog will be hungry and he will keep barking."

On hearing the hunter say this, the king was even more frightened than ever. It had never entered his thoughts that he had been doing anything wrong. He had thought that the people of his kingdom were simply supposed to always do exactly what he wanted. It had never occurred to him that a king should think of the happiness of anyone except himself.

He was now angry from his head to his feet, inside and outside. Either he would go mad hearing the continuous barking of that enormous dog, or else something would have to be done and that very quickly. So he called his wise advisors together and said, "What shall I do?"

The wise ones bowed their heads and walked off to think over the question together.

[*Leader: You may wish to pause here and ask the children what the king should do.*]

But try as hard as they could, the advisors could see only two possible solutions. Either the enormous dog must be killed or else every hungry person in the kingdom must be fed. No one was willing to kill the dog. So that meant there was only one thing left to do. Everybody in the kingdom must somehow be fed. The wise advisors were very clear in their minds about it. They returned to the king and told him plainly what had to be done. They had to shout, of course, because the enormous dog was still barking. The king hesitated no longer.

"Put all the servants on the palace grounds to work at once!" he commanded. "Go to the storerooms and get all the bags of rice you can find. Pile them high on carts. Take also meat from my cupboards and gather vegetables and fruits from my gardens. Send servants out with these loaded carts into all the towns and villages in my kingdom. Command the servants to find all the people who are hungry. Give them generously of these foods, and keep on giving food until not a single man, woman, or child in the land is hungry."

The advisors hurried away to do as their king commanded. Soon there was shouting and laughing, hustling and bustling all over the palace. In fact, the royal servants made so much noise that they could hardly hear the barking of the enormous dog. Presently a long line of carts, piled high with bags and baskets of food, rolled out through the palace gate. All day long, and day after day, the carts kept going until they had gone to every village in the land and food was taken to every house where somebody was hungry.

At last the day came when the enormous dog really stopped barking and lay down quietly beside the king's chair. The dog was satisfied. All the people inside the palace ground were happy and at peace in their minds. Everywhere in the land, the people were contented.

For the next few years the enormous dog stayed by the king's side to be sure the king never reverted to his old ways. A few times the dog barked to remind the king about justice, and each time the king remembered the important lesson he had learned.

Finally the dog was convinced the king truly understood the meaning of justice. One morning, she simply got up, walked out of the palace, and went to bark for justice in a new land.

30. Climb the Mountain for Heifer International

UU Principles 2, 5, 6, 7

Long-term / All ages / $

You will need:

- Computer with Internet connection
- Poster board, color markers, scissors, and glue sticks
- Money collection container

Before. Read stories online about how **Heifer International** helps people all over the world (**www.heifer.org**). Find fundraising ideas and resources such as the *Animal Crackers* guide, with activities and colorful animal fact cards you can use in a poster display. Download resources for free or have hard copies sent and pay only shipping.

The Project. Heifer International improves lives in rural areas around the world by providing animals that contribute to a family's sustenance and income. Share the stories of Heifer's impact. Talk about how and why this program resonates with Unitarian Universalist Principles. Do the families have a say in the help they receive (fifth Principle)? How does the project promote a fair and peaceful world (sixth Principle)? Plan a fundraising activity together and make a poster to advertise it. You might draw the slope of a mountain on poster board and show an animal figure climbing toward your fundraising goal.

After. Send funds you raise to Heifer International to purchase a flock of chicks ($20), a heifer ($500), or another animal for a family. Take a moment to acknowledge how your donation demonstrates the interconnectedness of all life on earth.

From *Wonderful Welcome* Session 7 (The Gift of Helping), Tapestry of Faith for grades K/1

31. Peace Pinwheel Vigil or Parade

UU Principles 2, 5, 6

Short-term / All ages / $

You will need:

- Paper, color markers, scissors, tape or glue sticks
- Straight pins and stiff straws or pencils with attached erasers for each pinwheel
- Large mural paper and bold color paints or thick markers
- Lyrics of songs about peace, from songbooks like *Singing the Living Tradition* (UUA, 1993), *Singing the Journey* (UUA, 2005), or *Rise Up Singing* (Sing Out Publications, 2004), or downloaded from the Internet

Before. Plan to stage or attend a peace vigil or parade in your community. Or set a half-day aside to make a peace display for your home's front yard, doorway, or windows. In advance, watch a short video on the website of Pinwheels for Peace (**www.pinwheelsfor peace.com/movie.mov**) that shows how to make a pinwheel from a square sheet of paper, a pencil or straw, and a straight pin . While online, read about the Peace One Day project to inspire your demonstration for peace. Look at songbooks such as *Rise Up Singing*, *Singing the Living Tradition* (the Unitarian Universalist hymnbook) and *Singing the Journey* (the UU hymnbook supplement), and plan to lead/teach peace songs. Choose a time and place for pinwheel and banner making that will facilitate conversation about peace—why it matters and what makes it so hard to achieve between people and between groups. Gather information to help you lead discussion and reflection at the vigil or parade about how a conflict currently in the news could be peacefully resolved.

The Project. Make pinwheels and a banner to display in a peace demonstration or on the outside of your home. Incorporate a hopeful message about peaceful resolution to a particular conflict or about peace in general. Explain that a vigil/parade/display for peace is a way to show what we believe. Point out that our second UU Principle lifts up justice and compassion in human relationships, and our sixth Principle extends these values and a wish for peace into the entire world community. Our fifth UU Principle encourages us to use the freedom democracy gives us to speak out.

Have everyone draw pictures or write words expressing their hopes and prayers for peace, and decorate a sheet of paper to cut and fold into a pinwheel. Find ways for each person to contribute to making a banner. Spend some time in silence and some time learning and singing peace songs. End the vigil or parade by sharing your hopes and prayers for peace while holding the pinwheels.

After. Initiate a conversation with children within a few days:

- What difference do you think our peace demonstration will make?
- Did you notice any reactions?
- Did anyone come forward to join you or to say they shared your wish for peace?
- Does taking action for peace make you feel more hopeful that it can happen? Why, or why not?

From *Faithful Journeys* Session 12 (Make Peace), Tapestry of Faith for grades 2/3

32. Fair Trade
Chocolate Sale with S'mores

UU Principles 2, 5, 6, 7

Long-term / All ages / $$

You will need:

- Fair trade chocolate
- Marshmallows and graham crackers
- A portable gas camping stove or an outdoor fire pit
- Skewers and paper napkins or plates

Before. Familiarize yourself with Global Exchange's fair trade chocolate campaign at **www.globalexchange.org**. Make note of such statements as "Most of the children who work without pay to harvest cocoa beans have never even tasted chocolate." A We Want More from Our S'mores event is one way to protest corporations' use of cocoa harvested by underpaid and unpaid workers, including enslaved children, in parts of Africa, Latin America, and Asia. Also visit the website of Fair Trade USA (**www.fairtradeusa. org**), the leading certifier of fair trade cocoa in the United States, to understand fair trade certification. For example, a fair trade label indicates that the chocolate was produced without child labor. Download information and images to share with your family or group, including a fair trade logo. Purchase fair trade–certified chocolate for s'mores and to sell. You might persuade a local supplier or retailer to donate chocolate bars or provide some to resell on consignment. For vegetarians, provide marshmallows made without animal products from a vendor such as Sweet and Sara (**http://sweetandsara.com**).

The Project. Work for justice by making a commitment to purchase fair trade when you buy chocolate and educate others to do the same. Stage a tasting and learning event for family, friends, and your neighbors, or bring fair trade s'mores to a community festival. You may wish to sell fair trade chocolate to raise funds for an antislavery or international child advocacy organization. Before publicizing the event, secure permits for an on-site open fire and permission to sell chocolate. Set up a table where visitors can learn why and how to buy fair trade chocolate. Display a pledge for visitors to sign: "I pledge to buy fair trade chocolate so cocoa farmers can build a future full of hope for their families!" Have copies of the pledge for people to take home. Provide sample letters for people to send to the makers of their favorite non–fair trade chocolates: "I am sad that cocoa farmers do not get paid enough and that sometimes child slaves are used to harvest cocoa instead of going to school. Please buy fair trade–certified cocoa so these problems won't happen anymore!"

After. Point out that purchasing fair trade chocolate is a way to exercise our fifth Principle, right of conscience. In this case, we protest child slavery and unfair compensation of cocoa farmers not by voting but by choosing where to spend our dollars. Make sure everyone knows that, although slavery is illegal everywhere in the world, it still exists. Even though children who harvest cocoa may be enslaved far away from where we live, our seventh Principle reminds us that we are all connected. To educate others to take action against modern-day slavery is not only a sign of our compassion and caring (second Principle) but also one way to affirm our sixth Principle, the goal of a just and equitable world community. What more can you do to fight modern-day slavery?

From *Love Will Guide Us* Session 15 (Love in Action), Tapestry of Faith for grades 2/3

33. Families Far and Near

UU Principles 4, 6, 7

Long-term / All ages / $$

You will need:

- Video recording and editing equipment

Before. Contact a local college's international student group or an organization that works with recent immigrants. Ask for individuals whom your family or group can interview about their travels to the United States. If individuals are not proficient English speakers, you will need an interpreter. Alternatively, arrange to interview a friend or community member who immigrated to the United States. Maybe a family member has an immigrant experience and would like to be interviewed. Plan a day, time, and place for the interview(s). Ask your subject for permission to edit the interview and share it publicly; if you interview minor children, ask a parent's or guardian's permission.

The Project. Together, generate questions for the interview and, if possible, offer the questions to your subject ahead of time. Questions could include:

- Where were you born?
- In what other countries have you lived?
- What would you like us to know about your family?
- What was your journey to the United States like?
- Did you bring family members with you?
- If you have family in another country, how do you stay in touch?
- What are some of your favorite memories of time spent with your family in your birth country?
- Which traditions from your birth country do you continue to keep, now that you live in the United States?

Before the interview, talk within your family or group about ways to demonstrate welcome to your subject(s) and gratitude for the opportunity to do the interview. Plan specific ways to be hospitable. Be aware of any young participant who is an immigrant or the child of a recent immigrant and how this activity might affect that youth.

After. Edit and share the footage from your interview. Could a local film festival or cable access television channel show your video? Post the video on a website such as YouTube. Discuss:

- What has the interview experience taught us?
- What more does it make us want to find out?

From *Families* Workshop 5 (Methods of Gathering Narratives and Texts), Tapestry of Faith for youth

34. One Laptop per Child

UU Principles 2, 4, 6

Long-term / All ages / $

Raise $199 for the nonprofit organization One Laptop Per Child (OLPC) (**http://one.laptop.org**) to help provide children in impoverished parts of the world a means to pursue our fourth Unitarian Universalist Principle—a free, responsible search for truth and meaning. Share examples of how computers and the Internet make learning and information more and more accessible to all members of your household. Ask:

- Is it fair that some schoolchildren have access to computers and the Internet for learning while others do not?
- What could be the consequences of not having these tools to help you learn?

When you reach across the interconnected web via OLPC, you help bring some of the world's poorest children a rugged, low-cost, low-power, connected laptop with software and educational content designed for cooperative, joyful learning. Local agencies and grassroots groups distribute OLPC's proprietary-design laptops to schoolchildren from Cameroon and Charlotte, North Carolina, to

Gaza, Nepal, and Paraguay, empowering them to learn and inquire on their own. Save together by placing a money container next to your home computer, or plan a fundraising activity such as a used-book sale. A computer retail or repair shop, a bookstore, or a school may allow you to collect money or hold a book sale or other fundraiser on-site. Discuss:

- What are your hopes for the donation you are making?
- How do you hope it will change a child's life?

From *Building Bridges* Workshop 16 (Evangelical Christianity), Tapestry of Faith for grades 8/9

35. Microlending Abroad

UU Principles 2, 5, 6

Long-term / All ages / $

One way to spread economic justice is to participate in international microfinance. A relatively small investment of U.S. dollars —say, $25—can capitalize an artisan or agricultural producer in a developing nation to start a business that can support that person and their family. When we help people help themselves, we create respectful, compassionate relationships grounded in our second UU Principle, which in turn advance the aims of our sixth Principle, a just and peaceful world community. On the website of Kiva (**www.kiva.org**), find descriptions of small businesses in such countries as Benin, Ecuador, and Palestine launched with loans from individual investors who have since been paid back. The website describes the projects of microentrepreneurs currently seeking loans. Through Kiva, you support an individual or a small collective to implement their own business plan and make a transformational, perhaps life-saving affirmation of our fifth Principle, that everyone should have a say in matters that concern them. Once you make a loan, you will receive payments up to the amount of your loan and the option to relend the money to another enterprise. Updates on the progress of a business you helped support will give you opportunities to revisit your involvement. Point out that a Kiva loan can transform someone's ability to improve their income and their life. How does it feel to think your faith in another person's capabilities can help improve circumstances for someone you may never meet? Do not emphasize that your loan, whatever its size, was a small amount. Not everyone in the United States has better access to bank loans than the microentrepreneurs who borrow through Kiva. Not everyone perceives $25 the same way. To children, youth, or adults who earn little money, $25 may seem a considerable amount. Take this opportunity to acknowledge different financial resources in your group and the wider world. Model gratitude by celebrating that your family or group is in a position to help others with a loan.

From *Riddle and Mystery* Session 2 (Religion to the Rescue), Tapestry of Faith for grade 6

36. Night Sky Adventure

UU Principles 4, 7

Short-term / All ages / $

"You have to have an alertness to deal with the unexpected. The history of science is filled with almost-made discoveries, missed by a hairline because . . . [someone] didn't have the alertness to realize they had a discovery."
—Clyde Tombaugh (1906-1997)

Clyde Tombaugh was an astronomer and a Unitarian Universalist who embodied our fourth Principle, a free and responsible search for truth and meaning. Our faith encourages us to ask questions, investigate the world, and be open to new information, ideas, and truths, as Tombaugh was when he discovered Pluto in the night sky in 1930—and as he probably would have been again had he lived to see Pluto's 2006 demotion to dwarf planet status. You need not be a family of astronomers to experience the vast oneness of our universe and to make your own discoveries in the night sky. Find a safe site that offers night access and a clear view. If an outdoor experience is not feasible, research stargazing events at local science museums, universities, or nature organizations, and arrange to attend a night hike, planetarium presentation, or astronomy or space exhibit. Bring a book or a phone app to help identify constellations. Encourage everyone to find their own images or patterns in the sky and come up with their own questions. Affirm that anytime we seek to learn or to help others learn by observing and asking questions, we act on our fourth Unitarian Universalist Principle. If anyone in your family or group is visually impaired, invite their observations and wonderings about night noises and other sensations under the canopy of night.

Ask:

- How does the night seem different from the daytime?
- What are the implications of the realization that all people exist under the same sky?

Consider expanding upon this experience by inviting participants to write a poem or essay about it. Maybe they want to reflect upon the oneness they experienced or their feelings about the infinite. Post the writings on your Facebook page or share them with friends. Ask, "How are these feelings reflected in the way you act in the world?" For example, feelings of oneness could lead to increased empathy or a desire to take better care of your little piece of the world through stewardship of the earth or being a good neighbor.

From *Faithful Journeys* Session 9 (Ask Questions), Tapestry of Faith for grades 2/3

More Projects for Families and Groups

This chapter will help you discover additional projects suitable and interesting for your family or group. It also introduces stories to inspire you to make a difference together and to encourage all of you, particularly young people, to take steps to change the world on your own.

The resources below will lead you into a world of seemingly infinite ideas for ecological stewardship, the promotion of local and global justice, and meaningful assistance to people near and far who need help; some suggestions will certainly appeal to you. However, simply performing a caring, useful act does not guarantee a spiritually transformative experience for you, your children, or your partners in action. Enhance any project that appeals to you with a plan that invites meaning making at every step.

Involve all potential participants, especially the youngest, in selecting a project. Make sure everyone has genuine interest in some aspect of it. Encourage individuals to articulate a call they hear to help solve a particular problem. Some may simply be eager to visit a new location, use a new tool, or meet new friends. That is okay. When you ask why a child wants to do an activity to help others or promote a good cause, you raise the expectation that this type of work has a purpose, and you affirm that the purpose may differ from one participant to another. Even though a child may not do so immediately, your question invites them to look inside for what that purpose might be—a lifelong faith development skill.

Apply a respectful, inclusive, and multicultural lens to any project you undertake. Remember to ask how you can help rather than assuming you already understand a problem and know the best way to ameliorate it. Take care to let partners in action and recipients of your service guide the way you speak about the challenges they face. Ask or wait for cues as to how children ought to behave in someone else's familiar space. Be explicit about the care you are taking to listen and learn before you act, to model respectful engagement.

After completing a project, give everyone in your family or group a structured opportunity to recall what they did, what they learned, and what they felt. Be ready to connect aspects of each person's experience with an element of faith that they already understand. Use value terms; point out that a child's action showed compassion, fairness, or empathy, and is a sign that they carry these important human values in their heart. Point out a positive effect of the action, even if it is a small one, and affirm that the world can be made a better place and the actions of people like them make it so.

Projects That Are Inclusive for Young Children

In many communities, it can be hard to find volunteer opportunities that are both open to young children and suitable for a multiage group to do together. These resources suggest ongoing, existing justice and service activities a family can join and projects to adapt and initiate from home.

Big-Hearted Families
www.bigheartedfamilies.org
The Big-Hearted Families website, a project of the organization Doing Good Together, displays the tagline "simple tools to grow big hearts." The "Pick a Project" pull-down menu allows you to browse projects by category (Advocate: Peace, Justice and Social Action; Provide Comfort; Adopt Holiday Traditions). Projects are presented with clear instruction steps, reflection questions, follow-up resources such as story and picture books, and extension activities.

Compassionate Kids

www.compassionatekids.com

A nonprofit organization founded in 2004 by Kelly Palmatier, a vegan, foster/adoptive, and homeschooling mom with a background in business and communications, Compassionate Kids offers free, printable activities from instructions for home composting to a one-page maze that teaches how to help homeless pets.

Doing Good Together

www.doinggoodtogether.org

This organization is dedicated to "helping people raise compassionate and socially conscious children through family volunteerism." Doing Good Together provides articles such as "10 Reasons Why Family Service Matters," a page of Family Stories, and a monthly compilation of family volunteer projects in the Twin Cities, Minnesota, metropolitan area.

Habitat for Humanity

www.habitat.org

This organization's Youth United program engages people ages five to twenty-five in planning, fundraising, and publicity to support the construction of new homes for people who need them in local communities. Ages sixteen and up are permitted to work on construction sites.

Kids Can Make a Difference

www.kidscanmakeadifference.org

This learning program for middle- and high-school youth lifts up the root causes of poverty and hunger while teaching that one person's help can make a difference. The page "What Kids Can Do" describes the purpose and the work involved in various categories of action (education, volunteering, giving testimony, fundraising) and provides many examples of actual projects done by children in fourth grade and up.

The New 50 Simple Things Kids Can Do to Save the Earth
(*EarthWorks Group, 2009*)

www.50simplekids.com

The updated best-selling book and new, colorful companion website for children present information, research tools, and a variety of short-term and more extensive learning and action projects for home or school use. The website's home page invites children to investigate why and how to protect or promote animals, energy, water, and recycling.

UNICEF

www.trickortreatforunicef.org

Money raised by children's annual Halloween trick-or-treating for the sponsored United Nations Children's Fund funds basic services such as nutrition, immunization, clean water, and education for children around the world.

The Unitarian Universalist Service Committee (UUSC)

www.uusc.org

UUSC advances human rights through grassroots collaboration. In fifteen countries throughout the world, UUSC fosters social justice and works toward a world free from oppression. UUSC's innovative approaches and measurable impact are grounded in the belief that all people have inherent power, dignity, and rights. Their yearly Guest at Your Table Campaign and service trips for youth and adults through the College of Social Justice are just a couple of ways families and multigenerational groups can join the UUSC in its work.

Inspiring Stories

Change the World Kids

www.changetheworldkids.org

In 2003, two eight-year-old girls in Woodstock, Vermont, learned about wars, earthquakes, and destruction of the earth's ecological balance around the world and were moved to help. They formed an action club whose young members help where help is needed and they are able, from shoveling snow and doing home repairs locally to selling fairly traded Costa Rican coffee and returning profits to farmers. Their motto is, "No one can do everything, but everyone can do something."

Craig Kielburger and Free the Children
www.freethechildren.com
Born in 1982, Craig Kielburger founded an organization with his brother Marc to fight child labor when he was twelve, after reading about a boy his age who had been enslaved in South Asia most of his life.

Generation Fix: Young Ideas for a Better World by Elizabeth Rusch (Beyond Words, 2013)
This book for ages eight and up includes stories of more than twenty young people who initiated projects for economic, environmental, and social justice, such as a large-scale collection of groceries for food pantries, the invention of a device to detect acid rain, and a protest for peace staged by elementary school students outside a high school that was prone to violence.

Giraffe Heroes Project
www.giraffe.org
This nonprofit organization maintains a website that "honors the risk-takers . . . who have the courage to stick their necks out for the common good." Stories can inspire children and adults to identify their own gifts and deep concerns, and use both to take action. The website features individuals of all ages engaged with a great variety of community and global problems. To avoid sharing descriptions of the world's worst violence with young children, search the Giraffe Hero database by "Age when commended"; select "youth (12 or less)."

International Children's Peace Prize
www.childrenspeaceprize.org
Presented each year since 2005 by a Nobel Peace Prize laureate on behalf of the Dutch organization KidsRights, the prize honors a child for dedication to children's rights. The 2013 award recognized Pakistan-born Malala Yousafzai, who began blogging for girls' education and has continued to risk her life to speak, even after being shot and critically wounded by a Taliban assassin at the age of fifteen. The website shares the stories of Yousafzai and previous young awardees, whose causes have included violence prevention in the slums of Rio de Janeiro, the rights of children with disabilities, and the basic needs of street children in Cavite City, Philippines.

TeenNick Halo Awards
www.teennick.com/shows/halo-awards/
This program, sponsored by the Nickelodeon television network, honors youth who are making a difference in their communities. You can read about them, watch the yearly award presentation, and nominate a youth for a Halo award.